George H. Horn

Synopsis of the Silphidae of the United States with reference to

the genera of other countries

George H. Horn

Synopsis of the Silphidae of the United States with reference to the genera of other countries

ISBN/EAN: 9783741129841

Manufactured in Europe, USA, Canada, Australia, Japa

Cover: Foto ©Thomas Meinert / pixelio.de

Manufactured and distributed by brebook publishing software
(www.brebook.com)

George H. Horn

Synopsis of the Silphidae of the United States with reference to the genera of other countries

Synopsis of the SILPHIDÆ of the United States with reference to the genera of other countries.

BY GEORGE H. HORN, M. D.

In its origin the present essay was intended to clear up some doubtful points which appeared to exist in our series of Catops. This required an examination of the genera into which it (or more properly Choleva), had been divided, and necessitated a determination of the question of the generic identity of the European and American Adelops. The investigation gradually extended from one genus to another until all the tribes were covered and almost unwillingly the species were passed in review, and the paper has grown to a size far beyond my first ideas. The door once open to foreign genera all have been included in the study and will be found in their places in the generic tables which follow, and in the event of any now unknown to us being discovered, their recognition will be made easy without the bibliographical research otherwise necessary. In dealing with genera foreign to our fauna it has not seemed necessary to do more than put them in their places, more would not be pertinent to the present essay. Figures in outline of all known genera (with few exceptions) have been given, nearly all of which have been drawn from nature. These it is hoped will prove of further assistance.

As might have been expected from an investigation of such a character, the number of exceptional cases to the generally accepted formula of the family has greatly increased. In order to call especial attention to some of these the formula is here repeated, and the exceptions indicated in as condensed a manner as possible.

SILPHIDÆ.

MENTUM quadrate or slightly transverse, sometimes slightly emarginate, frequently with a transverse piece between it and the ligula which is prominent, either emarginate or bilobed; mental suture distinct.

MAXILLÆ with two lobes, inner sometimes with a terminal hook (*Silpha*), the outer rarely slender and filiform (*Clambus*). Palpi four-jointed, the first joint always short, the others variable.

LABRUM usually visible, rarely almost entirely concealed (*Clambini*), of variable form, sometimes entire, usually emarginate or bilobed.

EYES oval or round, entire, usually finely granulated, coarsely in some Clambini.

ANTENNÆ variable in insertion, sometimes free at base (some Silphini and Cholevini), or under a frontal margin (Anisotomini), usually arising close to the eyes or distant from them (some *Silphæ* and in *Empelus* and *Calyptomerus*); usually eleven-jointed, rarely ten- or nine-jointed, the terminal joints either forming a club of variable structure, or gradually broader, rarely nearly filiform (*Pteroloma* and *Apatetica*).

PROTHORAX without distinct side pieces.

MESOSTERNUM short, side pieces closing the coxal cavities externally.

METASTERNUM usually large, truncate behind, short in the genera without eyes, side pieces distinct, the episterna long, epimera distinct, but in the Anisotomini partly concealed by the elytra.

ABDOMEN usually with six segments (seven in *Empelus*), rarely with five (*Sphærites, Lyrosoma, Colon, Clambus*), or even four (many females of *Colon*).

ANTERIOR COXÆ contiguous, conical, transverse at base and with trochantin, cylindric-conic and without trochantin in Cholevini; the coxal cavities strongly angulate externally (except Cholevini), and open behind in the first three tribes, closed in the others.

MIDDLE COXÆ not prominent, usually separated, rarely contiguous, oblique or transverse (*Clambus* and *Calyptomerus*), with distinct trochantin, the cavities closed externally by the mesosternal side pieces.

POSTERIOR COXÆ transverse, sometimes prominent internally (some Silphini), and in Clambini laminate, the plates more or less concealing the posterior legs.

LEGS often stout and fossorial or very slender; tibiæ usually with prominent terminal spurs which are rarely absent.

TARSI usually five-jointed, variable sexually or generically (Anisotomini, Cholevini), or four-jointed (Clambini).

ELYTRA usually entire, covering the abdomen, sometimes truncate (*Necrophorus*, some *Silpha, Sphærites* and *Apatetica*), epipleuræ distinct except in *Clambus* and *Calyptomerus*.

The above characters define, as far as it is possible in a general manner the present family, and the scheme seems principally noteworthy from the number of the exceptional cases, notwithstanding which the family seems to be as well defined an aggregate as very many of the families in the coleopterous series.

As constituted in the present essay the family differs in its composition from that at present given in the books. Lacordaire and Duval include *Leptinus*, the Catalogus (p. 741), adds *Sphærius*, and Leconte (Class. Col. N. A. pp. 48 and 52), adds *Brathinus* as a subfamily.

Regarding *Leptinus* I can only say that I fully agree with Leconte in separating it as a distinct family, and have nothing to add to the views expressed by him (Proc. Acad. 1866, p. 368), except that it seems more closely allied to this family than the Hydrophilidæ. I am not aware of any reason why *Sphærius* should be added and it seems that there are very many to the contrary, so that this does not seem to need discussion here.

The addition of *Brathinus* even as a subfamily introduces a very disturbing element to any system of classification, and after a careful examination I think the view originally expressed by Dr. Leconte (Proc. Acad. 1852, p. 150), is the correct one, and that the genus should take its place among the Scydmænidæ for the following reasons : The head is suddenly constricted behind to a neck which is gradually broader posteriorly, approaching the semiglobose form of *Scydmænus ;* the anterior coxæ are as in that genus and similarly with trochantin, the middle coxæ slightly prominent and separated, the posterior prominent, slightly transverse at base but contiguous, the trochanters oval, rather flat and not in the axis of the thighs and the elytra have no epipleuræ. The greater length of the maxillary palpi and the form of the hind coxæ have been urged as objections to placing *Brathinus* in Scydmænidæ. If the palpar character has any weight (and it seems to me to have no greater than generic value), the preponderance is greater against the Silphidæ than the Scydmænidæ. The structure of the hind coxæ seems to me essentially that of the latter family, the apparently transverse character being due to their contiguity. The absence of epipleuræ seems to be general in the Scydmænidæ. In *Brathinus* it will be observed that the first four abdominal segments have on each side near the posterior edge a deep setigerous puncture. I have not been able to assure myself that this occurs in the Scydmænidæ. Finally the general appearance of *Brathinus* is rather that of *Scydmænus* than of any Silphide, and the comparison of it with *Leptodirus* seems singularly inappropriate.

Having thus disposed of the genera which seem foreign to the family the arrangement of the others is the next subject of discussion. Here it is usual to review the modifications of the various parts of the external skeleton, but as most of the exceptional cases have already been given and as it is far more convenient to amplify under the tribal headings, it seems unnecessary to repeat them here, reserving for the present such remarks as may be proper to explain the reasons for the rejection of the old systems of classification and to defend that here proposed.

The family originally indicated by Latreille was more restricted than at present, and to Schiœdte is due the suggestion of adding the Anisotomini which had been considered a distinct family by Erichson and Stephens. Lacordaire divides the genera into three tribes in the following manner:

Posterior coxæ distant...*Leptoderides.*
Posterior coxæ contiguous.
    Posterior trochanters prominent...*Silphides.*
    Posterior trochanters placed in the axis of the thighs................*Anisotomides.*

Duval follows several years after with nearly the same system, separating the Clambites as a distinct tribe by the coxal plates.

The separation of Leptodirus in a distinct tribe by the distant posterior coxæ is certainly a very great exaggeration, and the character must be assigned rather a secondary rank in view of the fact that all the blind genera and Lyrosoma are so constructed. It is true that Pholeuon and Oryotus were unknown to the above authors or they would probably have seen the relationship existing between the three, as Schaufuss (Stettin Zeitsch. 1861, p. 424), did a few years after, although he appears to have overlooked entirely their resemblance to the Cholevini.

The value of the hind trochanters in separating the other two tribes is entirely illusory, in fact the character as made use of does not exist, and it seems to me remarkable that characters once suggested and gaining currency will often pass unquestioned, and be repeated from author to author until they become so fixed in the books that it is nearly impossible to free ourselves from them. Without desiring to cite numerous examples in proof of the assertion, the attention of students is invited to the trochanters themselves.

The next system of classification is that proposed by C. G. Thomson, (Skand. Col.). Here appears the first serious innovation and the first suggestions toward a rational arrangement. He recognizes fully the value of the structure of the anterior coxal cavities as a means toward that end, and it is to be regretted that the limited fauna of his country did not allow him to enter fully into the discussion of the subject. As it is the isolated character of his material has led him to make too many divisions and genera, a pardonable mistake for that reason. I cannot allow the present occasion to pass without special mention of C. G. Thomson's work. It is filled with important discoveries, new ideas and useful hints applicable to larger fields of study, and I am unable to understand why he appears to be so little appreciated by his European cotemporaries. With us it is usual before undertaking any work in which he has studied similar genera to refer to his book to avoid unnecessary labor, as it has more than once occurred to me to find characters already known to him which I had obtained after long and patient search.

The value of the coxal structure as a means of separating the family into tribes has already been intimated, and the following table is offered for the consideration of students.

Posterior coxæ simple.
  Anterior coxæ more or less transverse at base and with trochantin.
    Anterior coxal cavities open behind.
      Posterior coxæ contiguous..SILPHINI.
    Posterior coxæ separated.
      Anterior coxæ prominent. Abdomen with five segments...LYROSOMINI.
      Anterior coxæ not prominent. Abdomen with six segments...PINODYTINI.
    Anterior coxal cavities closed behind..............................ANISOTOMINI.
  Anterior coxæ cylindric-conic, without trochantin, the cavities closed behind
    often widely..CHOLEVINI.
Posterior coxæ laminate.
  Anterior coxæ with trochantin, the cavities closed behind...............CLAMBINI.

These characters are so easily expressed in words as to need no further comment, and under the descriptive remarks will be found comments on the various lines of affinity existing between the tribes.

In the tables of the genera of the various tribes will be found not only our own genera but all those described up to the present time, which are placed in position from an examination of the genera in nature with few exceptions.

For the types of many European genera I am indebted to M. Aug. Sallé of Paris, and Dr. Dohrn of Stettin. For the material for the elucidation of our own fauna outside of my own cabinet, I am indebted to Dr. Leconte, and Mr. Ulke of Washington, both of whom have allowed unrestricted use of their material. Nearly all the species described by Mannerheim, from Alaska, have been seen and described here from types sent by Mannerheim or Chaudoir to Dr. Leconte.

Before proceeding to the consideration of the tribes the following remarks on the geographical distribution of the genera may be of interest.

There are 43 genera recognized in the following pages distributed in the tribes as follows:

Silphini	8	of which there are new			1.
Lyrosomini	1	"	"	"	0.
Pinodytini	1	"	"	"	1.
Cholevini	16	"	"	"	2.
Anisotomini	14	"	"	"	1.
Clambini	3	"	"	"	0.

In the second tribe Lyrosoma has been revived from its improper suppression in Pteroloma. In the fourth tribe I have suggested the suppression of Drimeotus in Pholeuon, Catopomorphus in Ptomaphagus, Quæsticulus and Quæstus in Bathyscia; the last three had been suppressed in Adelops. With these explanations a concordance is established with the Catalogus, excluding Leptinus and Sphærius from the family. In addition to the new genera of the present paper six others have been published since the Catalogus.

Of the above genera

North America has represented	30.
Peculiar to North America	10.
Europe has represented	27.
Peculiar to Europe	10.
Common to Europe and North America	18.
Common to Alaska and Kamtschatka (*Lyrosoma*)	1.
Peculiar to India (*Apatetica*)	1.
Peculiar to New Zealand (*Camirus*)	1.
Peculiar to Madeira (*Stercus*)	1.
Peculiar to Brazil (*Scotocryptus*)	1.

By the above scheme it will be observed that the genera with four exceptions belong to Europe and North America, that each has nearly an equal number represented and with the same ratio of those peculiar to it.

The number of species described from Europe nearly doubles that from our own fauna.

Tribe I.—*Silphini.*

Anterior coxæ conical, prominent, contiguous, with large trochantin, the cavities strongly angulate externally and open behind, very widely in *Necrophorus* and *Silpha* and partially closed in the other genera. Middle coxæ widely separated in these two genera, narrowly separated or even contiguous in the others. Posterior coxæ contiguous. Abdomen with six segments except in *Sphærites*. Antennæ variably inserted, sometimes free at base or under a slight frontal margin.

The head is always free or nearly so and usually constricted behind into a neck. The antennæ are eleven-jointed in all except *Necrophorus* in which the true second joint is connate with the base of the third. The terminal four or five joints are usually thicker forming a club, abrupt and compact in *Sphærites*, abrupt but with mobile joints in *Necrophorus*, or elongate-oval and gradually formed in *Silpha*, etc. *Pteroloma* and *Apatetica* have slender antennæ, scarcely at all thickened externally. The eyes are at least of moderate size and often prominent, never absent. The thorax is variable. The elytra are distinctly margined at the sides, sometimes widely, the inflexed portion below the margin variable in width. This part is often erroneously called the epipleuron, it is more properly the epipleural fold, the epipleuræ proper being narrow portions along the extreme edge of the elytra. The abdomen is visible beyond the elytra in *Necrophorus*, *Sphærites*, *Apatetica*, and nearly all the species of *Silpha*, but entirely concealed in the other genera, the number of segments being six in all except *Sphærites* where there are but five. The legs are decidedly fossorial in *Necrophorus* alone, in the other genera rather slender. The tibiæ are nearly always spinulose externally, very indistinctly however in several genera. The tibial spurs are at least of moderate size. The anterior tarsi more or less dilated in the male.

This tribe contains all the large species of the family and none that are very small, its distinctive characters being the open anterior and the contiguous posterior coxæ. The next two tribes have the first of these characters but the hind coxæ are separated.

The genera here included seem quite homogeneous and form a natural series except as to *Sphærites*, which is somewhat aberrant by the abdomen and the compact antennal club. It seems however a link toward the Histeride series, while *Necrophorus* shows decided Staphylinide affinities.

Through *Pteroloma* and *Lyrosoma* as a further intermediate the tribe connects with the Cholevini, and by *Agyrtes* through *Pinodytes* with the Anisotomini.

Some authors have divided the tribe still further and have instituted tribes or families (Thomson), for *Sphærites* and *Agyrtes*. I can see no special advantage in such a course as the tribal distinctions must then be brought almost to a generic basis.

The following table gives in brief the important characters separating the genera.

Antennæ 10-jointed, capitate, the last four joints forming an abrupt club.
Middle coxæ widely separated. Anterior coxæ widely open behind
without post-coxal extcusion of the prothoracic epimera. (Pl. V,
fig. 2.)...**Necrophorus**.
Antennæ 11-jointed, either slender or gradually clavate.
Middle coxæ moderately separated. Anterior coxæ widely open behind with-
out post-coxal process of prothoracic epimera. (Pl. V, fig. 4 a.).
Silpha.
Middle coxæ narrowly separated or contiguous. Anterior coxæ narrowly
open, partially closed by a prolongation of the prothoracic epimera.
(Pl. V, fig. 6 a.).
Epipleural fold wide, the elytra margined at the sides. Last joint of
maxillary palpi slender.
Antennæ gradually clavate, not longer than the head and thorax.
Antennæ free at base, not inserted under a frontal margin, first and
and third joints long, the latter as long as the next two.
Necrophilus.
Antennæ arising under a frontal margin, first joint short, robust, third
scarcely longer than the second...............................**Pelates**.
Antennæ slender, scarcely thicker externally, as long as half the body.
Elytra entire; penultimate tarsal joint simple...........**Pteroloma**.
Elytra truncate; penultimate joint bilobed................**Apatetica**.
Epipleural fold narrow, the elytra with an extremely narrow margin. Last
joint of maxillary palpi ovate.........................**Agyrtes**.
Antennæ 11-jointed, capitate, the last three forming an abrupt club. Anterior
coxal cavities narrowly open behind, partially closed by a slender
prolongation of the epimera.
Abdomen with five segments. Elytra truncate.......................**Sphærites**.
Of the above genera *Apatetica* does not belong to our fauna, while
Pelates is thus far peculiar to it. *Necrophorus* and *Silpha* are widely
distributed, *Necrophilus* has one species on each side of the continent,
the other genera occur on the Pacific coast alone.

NECROPHORUS Fab.

Head large, suddenly narrowed in front of the eyes and also at a little distance behind them. Eyes large, oblique, moderately prominent. Labrum
transverse, deeply bilobed. Clypeus rhomboidal, separated from the front by
a fine suture and with a membranous rhinarium of variable size and shape.
Antennæ free at base, geniculated, apparently ten-jointed, terminated by an
abrupt four-jointed club, the first joint of which is glabrous, scape elongate
gradually clavate very nearly as long as the five following joints, second joint
longer than any of the following, joints 3—6 gradually shorter and broader;
the second and third joints of the club emarginate in front the last elevated in
an obtuse carina. Palpi short, the last joint cylindrical slightly acuminate at
tip, the penultimate obconical and stouter. Anterior coxæ conical, prominent
and contiguous with large trochantin, the cavities strongly angulate externally
and widely open behind, the post-coxal portion of the epimera short, broad
and obtuse. Middle coxæ widely separated. Posterior coxæ prominent, contiguous. Legs of moderate length, stout, the tibiæ broader at tip each with
two spurs of moderate length, the outer edge spinulose. Tarsi slender the

anterior dilated in the males and fimbriate at the sides. Thorax truncate in front, sides more or less margined. Elytra with distinct marginal line and with an epipleural fold of variable width usually wide, rarely narrow (*carolinus*). Metasternum moderately long, body winged. Abdomen of six distinct segments.

The head exhibits some variation in form within specific limits; that is, while the eyes in some individuals are very close to the hind angle of the head, in others the head is notably prolonged behind them. This is neither sexual nor specific.

The antennæ are always spoken of as ten-jointed but the true second joint appears as a node at the base of the one usually called the second. There is no variation in the form of joints 3—6 worthy of special mention. The club is slightly variable in the degree of the emargination of the second and third joints, so that the first and fourth joints meet when the club is closed in some species in others not. This character does not seem of any further value.

The clypeus is separated from the front by a fine suture and its anterior portion is membranous and may be orange-red or piceous, this portion is called the *rhinarium* and varies in size and shape but not sufficiently for use in the separation of the species.

The form of the thorax plays an important part in arranging the species in natural groups and requires special mention.

The first form or that which is most unlike all the others is that of *carolinus*. Here the thorax is oval not wider than long, narrowed behind, the lateral margin extremely narrow, the disc (for this genus), very convex and without any trace of the anterior sinuous impressed line. The punctuation is also peculiar. This form is called " oboval, not margined."

The second form is that represented by *americanus*, *orbicollis* and *Sayi*, in which the thorax is orbicular, truncate in front the sides arcuate and rather broadly margined. These species are moreover peculiar in having the elytra more oval and when we view the species from the side there seems to be a very distinct transverse depression of the elytra behind the base. The last two species above mentioned have erect hairs on the elytra. This form of thorax is called " orbicular."

The next form of thorax is that of *marginatus*, *obscurus* and *guttula*, called in the following pages "transversely cordate." The thorax is broader than long, the sides very narrowly margined and at middle sinuate. The anterior sinuous impression of the thorax is well marked.

The form in *pustulatus*, *vespilloides* and *tomentosus*, is called " trans-

versely oval," and resembles the orbiculate form but is shorter and
the sides at middle are either straight or slightly sinuate, the anterior
sinuous impression is usually deep and the disc of the thorax less
convex. The last named species is peculiar in having the thorax
densely clothed with yellow silken pubescence.

The elytra present but little that is peculiar except that mentioned
above. The sculpture is very little variable but the color very much
so in several species. The elytra have at the sides a marginal line
very distinct in all the species except *carolinus*. The part below this
line is called in the subsequent pages the "epipleural fold," and is
spoken of by most authors as the epipleuron but such is not the case,
the epipleuræ being extremely narrow pieces along the extreme edge
of the elytra. The marginal line varies in length in the species, in
some reaching from the outer apical angle nearly to the humeral
umbone, in others but half that length. The epipleural fold is
narrow in *carolinus*, wide in the other species.

The tibiæ vary also, the posterior pair being distinctly arcuate in
carolinus, marginatus, obscurus, orbicollis, americanus and *Sayi*, while
the last two have the middle tibiæ also curved. There has always
seemed to be great trouble in properly defining the limits of species,
and the numerous synonyms show how far separation has been pushed
on a color basis alone. Those which have no other claim to separation
their differences of color have been rejected and structural characters
taken as the basis of separation. Two species acknowledged in the
following pages are still doubtful in my mind but they are retained as
distinct for reasons given.

The following are the species recognized in the subsequent pages:

Group 1.—Thorax oboval, extremely narrowly margined, disc very unequally
                punctured, without anterior sinuous line.......**carolinus** Linn.
Group 2.—Thorax orbicular, sides and base with wide flattened margin, disc
                equally punctulate, sinuous line usually distinct.
        Elytra without erect hairs, disc of thorax red.
            Middle and posterior tibiæ arcuate.................................**americanus** Oliv.
        Elytra with erect hairs, disc of thorax black.
            Middle and posterior tibiæ arcuate..**Sayi** Lap.
            Tibiæ not arcuate...**orbicollis** Say.
Group 3.—Thorax transversely cordate, sides narrowly margined and sinuate
                at middle, anterior sinuous line distinct.
        Posterior tibiæ arcuate. Disc of thorax nearly smooth.
            First joint of club red..**marginatus** Fab.
            First joint of club piceous...**obscurus** Kby.
        Posterior tibiæ straight. Disc of thorax punctate.
            Antennal club and color of elytra very variable...**guttula** Motsch.

Group 4.—Thorax transversely oval, very little narrowed behind, sides and base broadly margined, the sides usually feebly arcuate or even slightly sinuate, anterior sinuous impression distinct. Tibiæ straight. Disc of thorax glabrous.
    Antennal club orange, first joint piceous.....**pustulatus** Hersch.
    Antennal club black.. ....**vespilloides** Hbst.
    Disc of thorax densely pubescent.
    Antennal club piceous.......................**tomentosus** Weber.

As our species are so few in number it has not been deemed necessary to reduce them to any tabular arrangement. To those who desire to make such a table the form of the tibiæ whether curved or straight will form a convenient point of departure.

N. carolinus Linn.—Form moderately elongate, head and thorax in repose rather strongly deflexed. Head black, shining, rather coarsely punctured, the lateral impressions moderately deep, rhinarium triangular, piceous. Antennæ black, the club entirely orange-red. Thorax oval as long as wide, narrowed behind, anterior angles broadly rounded, sides behind the middle slightly sinuate, base broadly arcuate, sides very narrowly margined, base more broadly, disc convex and without transverse impression, surface densely punctured in its apical third, more coarsely but less densely along the sides and base, the remainder of the disc shining and very sparsely punctate. Scutellum slightly convex posteriorly. Elytra not wider than the thorax and very little longer than wide, sides feebly divergent to the outer apical angle, apex squarely truncate, lateral marginal line very feebly elevated, the epipleural fold narrow, surface feebly shining, sparsely punctate and slightly wrinkled, color black, each elytron with small subhumeral spot, a subbasal fascia broadly interrupted at middle attaining the lateral margin and joining the humeral spot by a narrow line, near the apex a reniform spot which does not reach either the margin or suture. Abdomen above subopaque, sparsely punctate. Body beneath black, shining, metasternum with short yellowish hair. Middle and posterior tibiæ slender at base, rapidly broader toward the apex, the posterior arcuate in both sexes. The outer spur of the anterior tibiæ much stouter than the inner in both sexes. Length .80—1.12 inch; 20—28 mm. (Pl. V, fig. 1).

The male has the anterior tarsi dilated and the posterior femora stouter than in the female. The hind trochanter is prolonged in a short acute spine in both sexes.

This species is one of the most peculiar in our fauna. It seems to have shorter legs than the others, while the lateral marginal line of the elytra is scarcely prominent and the inflexed portion very narrow. Its markings are almost invariable.

Occurs in the Gulf States.

N. americanus Oliv.—Form robust, black, vertex, disc of thorax, two elytral fasciæ and epipleural fold, orange-red. Head almost impunctate, lateral impressions moderately deep enclosing the large orange-red space, rhinarium red. Antennæ black, club entirely orange-red. Thorax orbicular, truncate in front, wider than long, sides and base with a broad deplanate margin, disc

convex with scarcely a trace of the anterior sinuous line, surface smooth, a few
scattered punctures at the margin only, color orange-red, the flat margin black.
Scutellum flat. Elytra as wide as the thorax, about one-half longer than wide,
sides slightly arcuate, broadest a little behind the middle, then a little narrower
to apex which is sinuately truncate, lateral margin acute, moderately prominent, epipleural fold wide, disc broadly transversely impressed behind the
scutellum, then a little more convex and slightly declivous to apex, surface
sparsely indistinctly punctate: color black, epipleural fold entirely red, a post-
humeral broad red fascia interrupted at the suture and an apical fascia con-
sisting on each elytron of three confluent spots. Abdomen above sparsely
punctate, moderately shining. Body beneath black, shining, metasternum
with short yellowish hairs. The middle and posterior tibiæ are gradually
dilated to tip and slightly arcuate. The spurs of the anterior tibiæ are nearly
equal, the outer apical angle is however prolonged. Length 1.08—1.40 inch;
27—35 mm.

The males have the anterior tarsi broadly dilated and the posterior femora stout. The posterior trochanters are spiniform in both
sexes.

The color of the head and thorax serve to distinguish this species.
By the form of its thorax it is allied to *Sayi* and *orbicollis*. The
elytral markings are nearly constant, showing but little variation.

Widely distributed in the Atlantic region from the Middle States
to Texas.

N. orbicollis Say.—Form moderately robust, black, shining, elytra with
two incomplete fasciæ and short erect hairs. Head smooth, shining, sparsely
finely punctate, lateral impressions moderately deep, rhinarium orange-red.
Antennæ piceous, club orange-red with the first joint black. Thorax orbicular,
wider than long, apex truncate, sides and base nearly equally widely margined,
disc convex, median line and anterior sinuous impression moderately deep, the
flattened margin coarsely punctate and with a few erect hairs, the disc sparsely
minutely punctulate. Scutellum flat, moderately densely punctured. Elytra
not wider at base than the thorax, sides arcuate and gradually broader behind
the middle then slightly narrowed to apex which is sinuately truncate, disc
with vague transverse depression behind the scutellum then the surface is
slightly more convex and declivous to tip, surface shining, sparsely punctate
and with two vague costæ and with erect brownish hairs arising from each
puncture; marginal line moderately prominent, epipleural fold moderately
wide; color of elytra piceous black, with the post-humeral fascia broadly
interrupted by the suture and a subapical transversely oval spot orange-red,
epipleural fold piceous or black. Abdomen above sparsely punctate. Body
beneath sparsely punctate, metasternum with brownish yellow hairs. Middle
and posterior tibiæ in both sexes gradually broader to tip and straight.
Anterior tibiæ with equal spurs, the outer apical angle slightly prolonged.
Length .80—1.00 inch; 20—25 mm.

The anterior tarsi of the male are rather broadly dilated. The
hind trochanters are prolonged in both sexes. The posterior tibiæ
are much stouter in the male.

As in *americanus* and *Sayi* this species has the vague transverse impression of the elytra, and it further agrees with the latter in the presence of erect elytral hairs. From both these it differs in the straight tibiæ.

Widely distributed in the Atlantic region from Hudson's Bay southward.

N. Sayi Lap.—This species agrees in all the general characters of *orbicollis* except that the sides of the thorax are less arcuate, the epipleural fold of the elytra entirely orange-red and the middle and posterior tibiæ arcuate in both sexes. It is also generally smaller. Length .60—.80 inch : 15—20 mm.

Occurs in the northern part of the Atlantic region.

N. marginatus Fab.—Moderately elongate, black, elytra bifasciate with orange-red, epipleural fold red. Head minutely sparsely punctulate, lateral impressions moderate, rhinarium large red. Antennæ piceous, club entirely red. Thorax subcordate, broader than long, apex truncate, sides very narrowly margined, sinuate near the base, base arcuate, more broadly margined, margin punctured, disc convex very sparsely punctulate, median line obliterated, anterior transverse impression nearly so. Scutellum flat, sparsely punctate. Elytra not wider than the thorax, gradually wider from base toward apex, sides nearly straight, apex sinuately truncate, surface sparsely punctate and with feeble traces of two discal costæ; epipleural fold orange-red, disc with a rather broad, dentate. post-basal fascia usually entire, rarely divided at the suture, a second subapical often reaching the apical margin. Abdomen above and beneath sparsely punctate. Metasternum sparsely clothed with brownish pubescence. Anterior tibiæ with equal spurs, the outer apical angle moderately prolonged. Middle and hind tibiæ stout at tip, the posterior alone distinctly arcuate. Length .73—1.08 inch; 18—27 mm.

The males have the anterior tarsi dilated as usual and in both sexes the posterior trochanters are moderately prolonged, and the posterior tibiæ slightly pubescent on the inner edge.

The elytral markings vary a little in the width of the orange-red fasciæ, there are however no striking variations. The hind tibiæ being distinctly arcuate the relationship of this species is easily defined, and by the exclusion of *carolinus, americanus* and *Sayi*, by their peculiarities in other parts of the body we have *obscurus* alone with which it might be confounded.

Widely distributed, I have seen specimens from almost every part of our country, Pacific and Atlantic.

N. obscurus Kirby.—Closely allied to *marginatus* in form, color and markings, and differing as follows: Antennæ black, club red with the first joint black. Thorax with median line finely impressed, anterior transverse impression well marked. Posterior tibiæ very distinctly pubescent on the inner edge. Length 1.00 inch ; 25 mm.

The only constant character is that found in the club of the antenna, and it seems doubtful if this is sufficient to separate this and the preceding.

Occurs from Hudson's Bay to Canada and Utah.

N. guttula Motsch.—Form moderately elongate, black, elytra variable in color. Head rather coarsely punctured, lateral impressions moderately deep, rhinarium piceous. Antennæ black, the club orange-red with the first joint either piceous (*guttula*) or red (*Hecate*). Thorax transversely cordate, broader than long, apex truncate, sides sinuate posteriorly, base arcuate, margin narrow at the sides, a little wider at base, disc convex with the anterior transverse line deeply and the median line feebly impressed, surface moderately coarsely punctate but somewhat variable. Scutellum flat, moderately densely punctate. Elytra a little narrower at base than the thorax, gradually wider posteriorly, sides straight, apex sinuately truncate, surface moderately coarsely punctate with a few coarser punctures intermixed which in some specimens show a tendency to assume a seriate arrangement; color of surface very variable. Abdomen above and beneath moderately densely punctulate. Metasternum clothed with yellow silken hairs. Anterior tibiæ with nearly equal spurs, the outer apical angle slightly prolonged. Middle and posterior tibiæ gradually broader to tip, not arcuate. Length .52—.80 inch; 13—20 mm.

The color of the elytra is extremely variable in this species. In the typical form (*guttula*) the elytra are entirely black excepting a small subhumeral red spot. In these also the first joint of the club is piceous. A variety of this form occurs with a small red spot on the elytra posteriorly.

In the variety *Hecate* the elytra are fasciate after the style of *marginatus*, with the epipleuræ pale and the antennal club entirely red. The fasciæ are not constant in their width but become wide so as to be more or less confluent, so that in a specimen taken by me in company with the normal *guttula* the elytra have very little black on them.

The thorax varies in punctuation, being generally more coarsely punctured in the entirely black forms and more finely in the fasciate.

By the narrow side margin of its thorax this species must be associated with *marginatus*, from which it may always be distinguished by its straight tibiæ.

Occurs from Colorado to California, as far south as San Diego. It illustrates the tendency to melanism shown by many other species which extend from the Plains to California, and it may be here observed that the fauna of California often replaces a colored eastern species by one entirely black.

N. pustulatus Herschel.—Form moderately robust, piceous or black, elytra variable in color. Head sparsely finely punctate, rhinarium small, red. Antennæ piceous, club red with the first joint black. Thorax transversely oval, very little narrowed posteriorly, sides very slightly sinuate at middle, base subtruncate at middle, sides and base rather widely margined, disc moderately convex, anterior impression deep, median line fine, surface minutely punctate margin more coarsely. Scutellum densely punctulate at base. Elytra nearly as wide at the base as the thorax, slightly broader posteriorly with very feebly arcuate sides, apex sinuately truncate, surface somewhat variably but usually coarsely punctured and with two faint costæ and a few coarser punctures forming indistinct series. Abdomen above and beneath very sparsely punctate. Metasternum with brownish pubescence. The outer apical angle of the anterior tibiæ is moderately prolonged, the spurs are a little unequal, the outer larger. The middle and posterior tibiæ are gradually stouter to tip and straight. Length .80—1.00 inch; 20—25 mm.

This species exhibits a range of color variation of the elytra greater than any other species known to me.

N. nigrita Mann.—This form is entirely black and less shining than the others. The antennal club is red except the first joint.

Its distribution is from the middle of California southward to the Peninsula and Guadeloupe Island, thence eastward through Arizona to Texas.

N. pustulatus Herschel.—Here the elytra are black excepting a red spot of variable size at the side of the elytra at the usual position of the first band, and two spots posteriorly near the apical margin of variable size. The epipleural fold is black. This form is usually a little more coarsely punctured than the preceding. *N. tardus* Mann., is a synonym of this variety.

This form is the one occurring more especially in the Atlantic region from the New England States to Texas, where we find entirely black forms resembling *nigrita* in color and *pustulatus* in sculpture. It occurs also in Alaska.

N. Melsheimeri Kby.—Under this head are included those forms in which the epipleural fold is red, either entirely or in very great part. The variety most nearly approaching *pustulatus* has in addition the lateral spot of the latter species, while the small subapical spots are united in a narrow fascia. With this as a starting point we have the lateral spot extending forming a band of varying width and finally reaching the suture. The posterior band also becomes gradually wider so that we have forms in which the elytra are almost entirely red as in *guttula.*

This variety occurs from Colorado northward to the Hudson's Bay region and Alaska, thence southward through Oregon and the north of California.

In this species the series of variations in the color of the elytra may be made very complete, there being no link wanting either in this respect or in geographical distribution.

Occurs over the entire Continent north of Mexico.

N. vespilloides Herbst.—This species although quite distinct from the preceding presents but little that can be used in description to distinguish it. The only permanent character is the entirely black antennal club. It is always smaller and the surface much less sculptured. There are the same color varieties as in *pustulatus*, but I have never yet seen specimens entirely black or with entirely yellow side margin. Length .44—.60 inch ; 11—15 mm.

Occurs in Canada, and from thence westward to Oregon and Washington Territory and north to Alaska, also in northern Europe.

N. tomentosus Weber.—Moderately elongate, black, shining, elytra with two fasciæ and epipleural fold orange-red. Head shining, minutely punctulate, rhinarium large, red. Antennæ piceous, club black. Thorax broader than long, transversely cordiform, apex truncate, sides at middle slightly sinuate, base feebly arcuate, margin moderately wide, broader at the base, disc convex, surface punctate and moderately densely clothed with golden yellow hair. Scutellum flat, sparsely punctate. Elytra scarcely wider than the thorax, sides nearly straight and slightly divergent posteriorly, marginal line distinct but not prominent, apex sinuate truncate, epipleural fold wide, surface rather coarsely but not densely punctate and with two faint discal costæ; color piceous or black with two orange-red fasciæ, the post-humeral and sub-apical extending from the epipleural fold to the suture and rarely interrupted. Abdomen above densely punctured, beneath very sparsely punctulate. Metasternum clothed with golden yellow pubescence. Middle and posterior tibiæ gradually broader to tip, straight. Anterior tibiæ with equal spurs, the outer apical angle prolonged. Length .56—.80 inch ; 14—20 mm.

The anterior tarsi of the male are broadly dilated. The posterior trochanters are not much prolonged in either sex.

Widely distributed over the Atlantic region.

SILPHA Linn.

Head moderate in size, suddenly narrowed in front of the eyes except in *opaca* and *bituberosa* and somewhat narrowed behind except in these. Eyes oval, slightly oblique, not prominent except in *surinamensis*. Labrum transverse, variably emarginate. Antennæ free at base, inserted close to the anterior margin of the eye and distant from the frontal margin except in *opaca* and *bituberosa*, eleven-jointed, not geniculate, the last four or five forming an oblong club either loose or moderately compact. Palpi short, the last joint cylindrical obtuse at tip. Anterior coxæ conical, prominent, contiguous and with large trochantin, the cavities strongly angulate externally and widely open behind, the post-coxal portion of the epimera short and broad. Middle coxæ separated, widely in all the species except *opaca* and *bituberosa*. Posterior coxæ contiguous not very prominent. Legs moderate in length, the tibiæ slender, gradually broader to tip and spinulose externally. Anterior tarsi more or less dilated in the males. Thorax usually emarginate in front. Elytra margined, the margin more or less reflexed, the epipleural fold moderately wide more or less concave. Body winged, abdomen with six segments.

The head shows but little variation except that noted above. In all the species except *opaca* and *bituberosa* the eyes form the most prominent part of the sides of the head, but in these the head is slightly prolonged behind the eye and a little more prominent than it. In these also the muzzle is much shorter, and the antennæ are inserted close to the frontal margin and more distant from the eyes than in the others.

The antennæ are eleven-jointed and never elongate, the club is composed of four or five joints but in some species is so gradually formed as to make it difficult to determine whether it has the one or other number. The terminal joint of the club is flattened, oval at tip, but in *opaca* and *bituberosa* somewhat conical.

The thorax is variable in shape but is usually transverse, rarely orbicular (*surinamensis*), the apex emarginate more or less distinctly except in the two species above where it is truncate.

The elytra are costate in a variable degree in all except *truncata*, the lateral margin reflexed, the apex is variable, squarely truncate only in *truncata*.

The legs present but little of note other than some sexual variation which is given under the species.

The anterior tarsi of the male and in some species the middle also are dilated, while in some the dilatation is very feeble.

After a careful study of our species I can see no valid reason for adopting any of the genera into which the present has been divided. To those who desire to know more of these genera the more general works will give the desired information, and of these none is more worthy of attention than C. G. Thomson's Skandinaviens Coleoptera, a work on a small fauna, full of useful suggestions and giving evidence of careful and patient research.

The visibility of the prothoracic stigmata has been urged as a reason for the adoption of *Necrodes* as a valid genus, but as Lacordaire correctly remarks *S. americana* has the stigmate equally visible. From my observations on our species I am convinced that the visibility of the stigmate is merely an accident depending on the size and extent of the prothoracic epimeron, and the stigmate may be seen in any species in which the thorax is slightly bent upward so as to render the connecting membrane a little terse. I can see no reason for attaching any value to this character. It must be admitted that many of the characters separating the species of Silpha are such as might elsewhere be deemed of generic value, but from the standpoint of our fauna I can see no reason for admitting any other genus than Silpha.

Our species may be distinguished by the characters of the following table :

A.—Antennæ inserted close to the eyes and distant from the margin of the front. Middle coxæ widely separated.

Eyes large, prominent, posterior femora much stouter in the males.

surinamensis Fab.

Eyes not prominent, posterior femora similar in the sexes.

    Labrum broadly emarginate; third joint of antennæ as long or longer than the second.

      Elytra squarely truncate, similar in the sexes, surface not costate.

truncata Say.

      Elytra sinuate or oblique at tip, more prolonged in the female, surface distinctly costate.

        Thorax emarginate at middle of base, surface pubescent, posterior tibiæ of males straight.

          Intervals of elytral costæ tuberculate............**lapponica** Herbst.

          Intervals of costæ flat............................**trituberculata** Kby.

        Thorax arcuate or truncate at middle of base, surface not pubescent, posterior tibiæ male arcuate.

          Thorax entirely black..............................**inæqualis** Fab.

          Thorax bicolored..............................**noveboracensis** Forst.

    Labrum deeply emarginate, third joint of antennæ shorter than second, elytra with costæ often feeble the intervals with anastomosing lines.

      Form broadly oval, thorax reddish-yellow with discal black space.

americana Linn.

      Form oblong-oval, color above entirely black often with bronze surface lustre......................................**ramosa** Say.

B.—Antennæ inserted close to the margin of the front and more distant from the eyes. Middle coxæ rather narrowly separated. Posterior tibiæ of males unguiculate at tip. Labrum deeply emarginate.

    Form elongate-oval, (as in *trituberculata*).................**opaca** Linn.

    Form oval, (as in *ramosa*)..............................**bituberosa** Lec.

It may be here remarked that all our species occur in the region east of the Rocky Mountains. The Pacific coast has not yet furnished a species peculiar to it.

S. surinamensis Fab.—Form moderately elongate, depressed, piceous, elytra with subapical, narrow orange-red fascia often broken in spots sometimes wanting entirely. Head elongate-oval, sparsely finely punctulate, suddenly constricted behind the eyes and with a deep transverse occipital impression. Labrum broadly emarginate. Eyes large, oval, prominent. Antennæ with an elongated club of five loosely articulated joints, the last three pubescent. Thorax transversely oval, emarginate in front, sides and base regularly arcuate, . margin broadly flattened posteriorly, surface sparsely finely punctulate, at the sides and base more coarsely. Elytra as wide at base as the thorax, sides feebly arcuate and gradually broader posteriorly, apex obliquely truncate, more prolonged in the female, lateral margin acute, narrowly reflexed, disc flat, sides declivous, surface with three distinct costæ extending from the base to apex and a short humeral carina, at apical third between the outer costæ a tuberosity, intervals densely and moderately coarsely punctured with distant coarser punctures close to and on each side of the costæ, epipleural fold narrow. Body beneath sparsely punctate, clothed with brownish hair. Length * .64—.92 inch ; 16—23 mm. (Pl. V, fig. 2).

Male.—Anterior tarsi moderately dilated, anterior tibiæ slightly sinuous on the inner side, the femora with two teeth near the apex, one on each border, that in front larger. Middle tibiæ slightly arcuate. Posterior femora large, inflated and with a broad tooth near the tip on the posterior border, the tibiæ strongly arcuate with a triangular dilatation near the tip and the apical angle in front of the tarsi prolonged. Apex of elytra obliquely truncate but not prolonged.

Female.—The anterior tarsi are slender, the tibiæ not sinuous, the femora without teeth. The middle tibiæ are slightly arcuate. The posterior femora are slender and simple and the tibiæ nearly straight, the apex not prolonged in front of the tarsi. The elytra are more obliquely prolonged.

Males occasionally occur with the sexual characters almost entirely undeveloped, differing in no respect from the female except that the anterior tarsi are feebly dilated and the tip of the posterior tibia is prolonged in front.

This species is the nearest approach in many respects to Necrophorus, and the discal elevation of the thorax is a feeble imitation of that genus.

Widely distributed in the Atlantic region.

S. truncata Say.—Moderately elongate, black, depressed, surface sparsely clothed with fine black pubescence. Head moderately constricted behind the eyes, the occiput transversely impressed, surface densely punctured and finely pubescent. Labrum broadly emarginate. Antennæ black, club elongate-oval, of five joints, the first two glabrous, the terminal one-half longer than the tenth. Thorax one-third wider at base than long, narrowed in front, apex feebly emarginate, sides slightly arcuate, basal angles obtuse, base trisinuate, disc moderately convex, sides posteriorly vaguely deplanate, surface densely punctured and finely pubescent. Scutellum densely punctured. Elytra as wide at base as the thorax, slightly wider posteriorly, sides feebly arcuate, margin narrowly reflexed, apex squarely truncate, disc rather flat, sides gradually arcuate, surface subopaque sparsely punctulate and pubescent, sometimes with faint traces of the two inner costæ and a slight tuberosity. Abdomen above densely, beneath more sparsely punctate and pubescent. Body beneath moderately densely punctured. Epipleural fold of elytra rather narrow. Length .50—.60 inch : 12.5—15 mm.

The male has the anterior tarsi moderately dilated and the abdomen much more prolonged beyond the elytra than the female.

---

* These measurements are taken from the head to the tip of the elytra, the abdomen being so variably retracted or protruded as to give unreliable measures. This course is followed in all the species of this genus.

This species is easily known by its very black velvety aspect with the elytra feebly sculptured and squarely truncate at apex.

Occurs in Kansas, New Mexico and Arizona.

S. lapponica Herbst.—Oval, slightly oblong, depressed, black opaque, head and thorax pubescent. Head densely punctured with short erect yellow hairs. Labrum broadly emarginate. Eyes oval, oblique, not prominent. Antennæ black with an oval club of four joints, the first glabrous, the terminal longer. Thorax nearly twice as wide as long, sides arcuate and gradually narrowed to the front, apical and basal angles obtuse, base feebly emarginate at middle, on each side sinuate, disc irregular with vague tuberosities clothed with darker pubescence, surface densely punctured and clothed with short yellowish pubescence. Scutellum densely punctured. Elytra as wide as the thorax, sides nearly parallel or very feebly arcuate, the margin moderately reflexed, apex sinuately truncate, more prolonged in the female, disc flat, sides declivous, surface tricostate, the outer shorter but more elevated terminating at a tuberosity, second and third feebler but gradually longer, the intervals with a row of moderately large tubercles between which the surface is obsoletely punctate and with very short hairs; epipleural fold moderately wide, concave. Body beneath moderately densely punctate and clothed with brownish hairs. Length .48 inch; 12 mm.

In the male the first four joints of the anterior tarsi are moderately dilated. In the female the sutural angle of the elytra is much more prolonged than in the male.

The species varies in length a little larger or smaller from the above measurement. It is an easily known species.

Occurs from western Canada to Alaska, thence southward through Oregon and California to Mexico, also in the region of the Plains. I have not seen it from the region east of the Mississippi.

S. trituberculata Kby.—Oblong-oval, black, sparsely clothed with very short hair. Head moderately narrowed behind the eyes, occipital impression rather deep, surface densely punctate. Labrum short, broadly emarginate. Antennæ black, with four-jointed club, the terminal joint nearly as long as the preceding two. Thorax about one and a half times as broad as long, narrowed in front, sides moderately arcuate, base emarginate at middle, sinuate each side, disc moderately convex with somewhat irregular surface, the sides slightly flattened, surface densely punctured and with short pubescence. Scutellum flat moderately densely punctate. Elytra as wide as the thorax and twice as long, sides nearly straight, margin narrowly reflexed, apices in male conjointly rounded, in female slightly sinuate and prolonged, surface coarsely but not densely punctate, each puncture with a short recumbent hair, disc flat at sides rather suddenly declivous and with three distinct costæ, the outer more elevated terminating at the tuberosity, the middle passing through the tuberosity and often reaching the apex very nearly, the inner nearly reaching the apex. Body beneath black, shining, moderately densely punctate. Length .36—.44 inch; 9—11 mm.

The anterior tarsi of the male are moderately dilated, the posterior tibiæ straight.

In some specimens the two inner costæ of the elytra are interrupted near their apices and reappear near the apical margin as small oblong tubercles, these two with the usual tuberosity gave to Kirby the specific name. This species is the smallest in our fauna and resembles a miniature *inæqualis*, but is more elongate and with the base of the thorax emarginate at middle. It also resembles *opaca*, but the differences are still more important as will be seen under that species.

Occurs in the Hudson's Bay region.

S. inæqualis Fabr.—Oval, slightly oblong, depressed, black, opaque. Head gradually narrowed behind the eyes, occiput slightly transversely impressed, surface moderately densely punctured. Labrum broadly emarginate. Antennæ black, rather short, club gradually formed of four joints the terminal longer. Thorax twice as wide as long, narrowed in front, apex emarginate, sides moderately arcuate, hind angles obtuse, base with a broad truncate lobe at middle on each side sinuate, disc at middle with feebly elevated longitudinal costæ, the two at middle nearly straight, the outer two sinuate, surface more densely punctured at middle than at the sides. Scutellum broad acute at tip, densely punctured. Elytra as wide as the thorax, very little longer than wide conjointly, sides moderately arcuate, margin broad and rather widely reflexed, apices conjointly rounded in the male, slightly obliquely prolonged in the female, disc flat at middle, obliquely declivous at the sides, with three costæ, the outer stronger and terminating one-third from apex in a slight tuberosity, the two inner costæ very feebly elevated, attaining the apical margin, intervals obsoletely sparsely punctate. Epipleural fold broad, its inner portion vertical. Body beneath more shining than above, sparsely punctate and pubescent. Length .40—.56 inch; 10—14 mm.

In this species the anterior tarsi of the male are but feebly dilated, the tips of the elytra conjointly rounded. In the female the elytra are obliquely prolonged and the margin slightly sinuate near the tip.

This species could hardly be mistaken for any other species excepting possibly *trituberculata*, which is however more elongate, the lobe of the thorax emarginate and the anterior tarsi of the male very distinctly dilated. Immature specimens at times resemble *marginalis*, but this species is always more elongate and the elytra more coarsely punctured.

Widely distributed over the Atlantic region east of the Rocky Mts.

S. noveboracensis Forst.—Oval, slightly oblong, beneath nearly black, thorax piceous broadly margined with yellow, elytra brownish to piceous. Head moderately densely punctate, occiput feebly transversely impressed. Labrum moderately deeply emarginate. Antennæ with four-jointed, elongate-oval club, the terminal joint longer. Thorax about one-half wider than long, narrowed in front, apex emarginate, sides moderately arcuate, the extreme margin slightly thickened, base truncate at middle, sinuate each side, disc moderately convex, sides broadly flattened, the former with slightly irregular

surface, punctuation moderately dense but not deeply impressed. Scutellum
flat, densely punctured. Elytra as broad as the thorax, sides slightly arcuate,
margin moderately wide and reflexed, apices conjointly rounded in the male
and slightly prolonged in the female, surface very distinctly and moderately
densely punctate, a slight tuberosity posteriorly through which two of the
costæ pass, the inner costa is fine and entire extending from base to apical
margin, the middle is obliterated at its basal third but attains the apex, the
outer and stronger costa extends from the humeral umbone and after passing
through the tuberosity joins the second costa. Epipleural fold moderately
wide, concave. Body beneath moderately densely punctate and clothed with
short brownish hair. Length .52 inch; 13 mm.

The males have the anterior tarsi very little broader than the female.
In both sexes the posterior tibiæ are arcuate, more distinctly in the
male. The junction of the outer and second costa is not always abso-
lute, although in the vast majority there is a much closer approximation
than in any other of our species.

Widely distributed in the Atlantic region east of the Rocky Mts.

S. americana Linn.—Broadly oval, depressed, beneath black, thorax
yellow with discal black space, elytra brownish with the elevations darker.
Head gradually narrowed behind the eyes, occiput transversely impressed,
surface moderately densely punctured, sparsely pubescent. Antennæ rather
short, club gradually formed of five joints the last three pubescent, the terminal
longer. Labrum deeply emarginate. Thorax nearly twice as wide as long,
much narrowed in front, apex emarginate, sides feebly arcuate, hind angles
obtuse, base broadly lobed at middle, sinuate each side, surface densely and
equally punctured. Scutellum broad, densely punctured. Elytra a little wider
than the thorax, in some specimens wider conjointly than long, sides moderately arcuate, margin broad, apices variable in the sexes, disc feebly convex
with three very indistinct costæ between which are anastomosing elevations,
the intervals moderately densely punctate. Epipleural fold broad, its inner
portion vertical. Body beneath black, moderately densely punctate. Length
.64—.80 inch; 16—20 mm.

In the males the anterior and middle tarsi are moderately and
similarly dilated, the elytra are always shorter and more obtuse at
tip, the sutural angle is slightly retracted but acute. In the female
the tarsi are not dilated, the elytra more obliquely prolonged and the
suture more distinctly retracted.

Occurs everywhere from Hudson's Bay to Texas, and to the eastward of that line.

I have adopted the Linnean name for this species in preference to
that of Catesby, whose name was published in 1731, prior to any of
the dates accepted as the starting point of our nomenclature and as
stated by Crotch the use of a binomial designation, for this species
was merely accidental, as Catesby had at that time no idea of the
binomial system subsequently proposed by Linnæus.

S. ramosa Say.—Oblong-oval, depressed, black, elytra varying from opaque black to slightly bronze, without pubescence. Head oval, very little narrowed behind the eyes, which are feebly prominent, surface densely punctured, smoother in front. Labrum deeply emarginate. Antennæ with an elongate-oval club of four joints, the last three pubescent, the terminal longer. Thorax about one-half wider than long, sides arcuate and gradually narrowing to the front, the margin with a smooth narrow thickened edge, apex feebly emarginate, the angles obtuse, base bisinuate with obtuse angles, disc feebly convex, very densely and evenly punctured. Scutellum densely punctured. Elytra as wide as the thorax, sides parallel or feebly arcuate, the margin reflexed but of variable width, apices conjointly rounded in the male or slightly obliquely prolonged in the female, disc regularly convex, sides not declivous, surface with three smooth irregular costæ, feebly elevated with anastomosing branches from one to the other, the intervals opaque from an extremely fine granulation and with punctures moderately densely placed; epipleural fold moderately wide, concave. Body beneath sparsely punctate and with short, sparse, brown hair. Length .48—.70 inch; 12—18 mm.

In the male the anterior and middle tarsi are both dilated the former a little more broadly. In the female the tarsi are slender and the elytra a little more prolonged.

In the wide extent of country over which this species is distributed there is a certain amount of variation of form and surface lustre. This has already been noticed by Dr. Leconte. (Proc. Acad. 1853, p. 279), and requires no further mention here than to state that more broadly oval forms occur with the margin more widely reflexed, these are usually more opaque. The more oblong forms with the margin less widely reflexed are more shining and have often a distinct æneous surface lustre.

Occurs from Wisconsin westward to Oregon and California, and southwesterly to Nebraska, New Mexico and Arizona.

S. opaca Linn.—Oblong-oval, blackish, opaque, sparsely clothed with short yellowish hair. Head short, a little broader behind the eyes then slightly narrowed without occipital impression, surface densely punctured, clypeus short, antennal fovea intermediate between the frontal margin and the eye. Labrum deeply triangularly emarginate. Antennæ black, not thick, the four joints of the club not very much wider, the terminal conical at tip as long as the two preceding together. Thorax very nearly twice as wide as long, slightly narrowed in front, sides rather broadly arcuate, base broadly lobed at middle on each side sinuate, disc at middle slightly more convex and somewhat irregular, at sides somewhat flattened surface densely punctured often with some smoother spaces at middle. Scutellum flat, densely punctured. Elytra not wider than the thorax, a little more than twice as wide as long, sides very little arcuate, the margin narrowly reflexed, apices conjointly rounded in both sexes, surface moderately densely punctate, each puncture with a short yellowish hair, disc flat at middle, declivous at the sides with three costæ, the outer more elevated terminating posteriorly in a well-marked tuberosity, the middle nearly obliterated at the base, passing the inner side of the tuberosity and slightly sinuous extending very nearly to the apical margin, the inner costa more distinct than the middle and less prolonged at tip. Body beneath black, shining, not densely punctate. Length .44 inch; 11 mm.

The anterior tarsi of the male are moderately, the middle tarsi less dilated. The posterior tibiæ are slightly arcuate and at the inner apical angle is a short brush of hairs behind which is a distinct hook-like process arising from the inner side of the tibia and curving forward. The tibial spurs are exterior to this hook. In the female the tarsi are slender and the hind tibiæ without the brush of hairs and the hook.

The shorter head and the insertion of the antennæ so much closer to the frontal margin, the similarity of the elytral apices in the sexes and the peculiar hook on the hind tibia of the male, mark this and the next species as very distinct from all the others in the genus in our fauna. By these characters the species is abundantly distinguished from *trituberculata* which it resembles in a general way.

I have seen but two specimens collected in our territory, one from Hudson's Bay, the second from near Mono Lake, California, which is more decidedly black.

S. bituberosa Lec.—Form oval, very slightly oblong, black opaque, sparsely clothed with very short hair. Head short, densely punctured, formed as in *opaca*. Labrum as in *opaca*. Antennæ with four-jointed club, more abruptly formed than in *opaca*, the terminal joint nearly as long as the preceding two and conical at tip. Thorax twice as wide as long, very little narrowed in front, apex truncate, sides broadly arcuate, base with median lobe truncate, on each side arcuate, disc slightly more convex at middle, sides feebly flattened, surface densely punctured without smooth spaces. Scutellum flat, very densely punctured. Elytra as wide as the thorax and twice as long, sides moderately arcuate, margin moderately reflexed, more widely near the base, apices conjointly rounded in both sexes, surface densely and coarsely punctate, each puncture with a very short hair, disc flat or very slightly convex, the sides declivous, surface tricostate, the outer costa stronger and terminating at the moderately developed tuberosity, the middle costa feeble at base, slightly curved at the tip but not attaining the apical margin, the inner costa shorter than the middle. Body beneath black, not very densely punctate. Length .48 inch; 12 mm. (Pl. V, fig. 4).

The sexual characters here are precisely as in *opaca* which it otherwise greatly resembles. It is however a much broader species and in form more nearly resembles *inæqualis*. It will be observed also that these two species *opaca* and *bituberosa* have the middle coxæ more closely approximated than in any other of our species, and in the former might be called rather narrowly separated.

Occurs from northern Kansas to Wyoming and Montana.

NECROPHILUS Latr.

Head oval, not narrowed behind the eyes which are round and moderately prominent. Labrum transverse, feebly emarginate. Antennæ free at base, nearly reaching the base of the thorax, slightly geniculate, first joint moderate in length, a little stouter toward the tip, second half as long and more slender, third as long as the first, slightly curved, gradually stouter to tip, 4—5—6 gradually shorter, together about one-half longer than the third, last five joints forming a loose club, seventh joint conical, joints 8—10 broader than long, eleventh oval, pointed at tip, the first six joints glabrous, shining, last five punctured and finely pubescent. Maxillary palpi moderately long, first joint very short, second slender at base gradually thicker, third half as long as second, obconical, fourth cylindrical as long as second pointed at tip. Anterior coxal cavities open behind, partially closed by a slender prolongation of the epimera. Middle coxæ narrowly separated, posterior coxæ contiguous. Legs moderately long, anterior and middle tibiæ with short ciliæ externally, the posterior very feebly spinulose. Tarsi slender, the anterior and middle equally dilated in the male. Thorax emarginate in front, lateral margin explanate and translucent. Elytra margined, epipleuræ broad. Form rather broadly oval. Body apterous (metasternum short) *Pettitii*, winged (metasternum long) *hydrophiloides*.

Two species are known in our fauna as follows:

Body apterous, elytra suddenly declivous posteriorly, the stria feeble, the punctures large..................... ....**Pettitii** n. sp.
Body winged, elytra gradually declivous, striæ moderately deep, the punctures fine.......... .... **hydrophiloides** Mann.

N. Pettitii n. sp.—Broadly oval, narrower in front, dark chestnut-brown, shining, glabrous. Head sparsely, finely punctulate. Thorax nearly twice as wide at base as long at middle, a little wider in front of base, sides arcuate, gradually narrowed to the front, margin broadly explanate, flat, translucent, disc more convex, apex emarginate, base squarely truncate, apical angles slightly obtuse, hind angles nearly rectangular, surface very sparsely punctate, very finely at middle, more coarsely at the sides. Elytra oval, disc suddenly declivous at apex, very little longer than wide, base truncate, wider than the elytra, humeri moderately prominent, obtusely rectangular, margin moderately wide, surface with rows of coarse, deep punctures, moderately closely placed, the intervals between the rows, convex, alternately a little more so, smooth. Body beneath very sparsely punctate, abdomen smooth. Femora very sparsely punctate. Length .44 inch; 11 mm.

In the males the first four joints of the anterior and middle tarsi are feebly dilated. The body is apterous.

This is the species erroneously determined by me (Trans. Am. Ent. Soc. 1868, p. 125), as *subterraneus*, from which this species differs in its much broader form, larger size and the posterior legs similar in the two sexes. The European species is also apterous.

Occurs from Canada (Pettit), to Kentucky (Dury).

N. hydrophiloides Mann.—Oval, slightly oblong, a little narrowed in front, piceous or nearly black, margins paler, surface shining. Head sparsely punctulate. Thorax transverse, twice as wide as long, narrowed in front, widest a little in front of base, sides arcuate, margin broadly explanate, translucent, apex moderately emarginate, the angles very obtuse, base feebly bisinuate, angles rounded, disc convex sparsely punctate, margin a little more coarsely. Elytra oval, broadest at middle, not wider at base than the thorax, base oblique on each side, humeri obtuse, margin moderately wide, surface moderately deeply striate, striæ rather finely crenately punctured, intervals convex smooth. Body beneath and abdomen nearly smooth. Femora with very few punctures. Body winged. Length .36—.44 inch; 9—11 mm. (Pl. V, fig. 5).

The males have the first three joints of the anterior and middle tarsi broadly dilated, the fourth joint less so. This species is more elongate than the preceding and has the elytral margin less developed.

Occurs from Alaska southward through California.

PELATES n. g.

Head broadly oval, very slightly narrowed behind the eyes, the latter round, moderately prominent. Labrum short, transverse, feebly emarginate. Maxillary palpi moderate in length, first joint very short, second slender, cylindrical, third shorter obconical, fourth longer than the second, cylindrical, acute at tip. Antennæ a little longer than the head and thorax, gradually clavate, inserted under a distinct frontal margin, first joint stouter cylindrical, suddenly narrowed at base, joints 2—7 obconical, the third a little longer, 8—11 a little broader, the last elongate oval, pointed at tip. Anterior coxal cavities partly closed behind by a slender prolongation of the epimera. Middle coxæ very narrowly separated. Posterior coxæ contiguous. Legs rather short, the tibiæ scarcely at all spinulose externally. Tarsi slender. Elytra rather widely margined, the epipleuræ wide. Form broadly oval, subdepressed as in *Peltis*, body winged.

This genus, for which I have adopted an unpublished name of Fischer, is closely allied to Necrophilus but differs especially in the characters given in the table, and also by the anterior tarsi alone of the male feebly dilated.

P. latus Mann. (*Necrophilus*).—Broadly oval, about one-half longer than wide, feebly convex, piceous or castaneous, margins paler, surface glabrous, shining. Head sparsely irregularly punctate. Thorax twice as wide as long, narrower in front, sides moderately arcuate from base to apex, margin moderately explanate, apical angles rounded, hind angles obtuse, apex emarginate, base truncate. Elytra as wide at base as the thorax, sides feebly arcuate, margin moderately explanate and slightly reflexed, surface striate, striæ moderately coarsely punctured, intervals flat, smooth. Body beneath coarsely but sparsely punctate, femora punctate. Length .14—.16 inch; 3.5—4 mm. (Pl. V, fig. 6).

This insect resembles somewhat in form *Peltis ferruginea*, but is much smaller and a little more convex.

Occurs from Alaska to Washington Territory.

PTEROLOMA Gyll.

Head oval, gradually but feebly narrowed behind the eyes which are round and moderately prominent. Labrum transverse, emarginate. Maxillary palpi moderately long, rather slender, first joint very short, the next three nearly equal, the second being slightly conical, the fourth acute at tip. Antennæ slender, as long as half the body, base free, very little thickened toward the tip, first joint rather short, stouter than the following, second a little shorter than the first, third longer, joints 3—10 very gradually decreasing in length, eleventh a little longer than the tenth, oval and acute at tip. Anterior coxal cavities partly closed behind by a slender prolongation of the epimera. Middle coxæ oval, not prominent, narrowly separated, posterior coxæ contiguous. Legs slender and long, tibiæ slender not or extremely feebly spinulose externally. Tarsi slender. Elytra margined, epipleuræ moderately wide. Form elongate with Carabide facies.

This genus is remarkable in the present tribe in the absence of tibial spinules and the slender elongate antennæ. Two species occur in our fauna both having considerable resemblance to Carabidæ so that the genus had been placed in that family, *P. Forsstrœmii* resembling a Nebria while *tenuicorne* recalls Calathus.

The two species are as follows:

Thorax cordiform, base narrowed......................................**Forsstrœmii** Gyll.
Thorax transverse, base not narrowed, gradually narrowed in front.
                                               tenuicorne Lec.

P. Forsstrœmii Gyll.—Moderately elongate, piceous, elytra, antennæ and legs paler, surface moderately shining, glabrous. Head coarsely irregularly punctured, a vague vertical fovea. Thorax cordate, one-half wider than long, sides arcuate in front, sinuate posteriorly, margin acute, slightly reflexed, apex emarginate, apical angles obtuse, basal angles rectangular, base truncate a little wider than the length of the thorax, an intra-angular impression, surface coarsely but irregularly punctured, median line moderately impressed foveate posteriorly. Elytra wider than the thorax, oval, narrower posteriorly, humeral angles obtuse, disc moderately convex, surface deeply striate, striæ coarsely punctured, intervals convex, the third and fifth with distant coarse punctures. Epipleuræ very coarsely punctured. Body beneath sparsely and indistinctly punctured. Length .24 inch; 6 mm.

The males have the anterior tarsi feebly dilated, and the first two joints of the middle a little stouter than in the female, in the latter sex the sixth ventral segment is deeply longitudinally impressed.

The resemblance of this insect to a small Nebria or to a Loricera is remarkable, and the deep punctures of the alternate intervals of the elytra are repeated here.

Occurs from the north of Europe through Asia to Alaska.

P. tenuicorne Lec. (*Necrophilus*).—Oblong-oval, piceous or castaneous, feebly shining, glabrous. Head nearly smooth. Thorax one and a half times as wide as long, widest at the middle, sides feebly arcuate, apex emarginate, a little narrower than the base, apical angles obtuse, base truncate, hind angles

rectangular or slightly obtuse, margin explanate, more widely flattened posteriorly, surface feebly convex, variably punctured, sometimes very indistinctly
or again with evident punctures at the sides and base. Elytra oval, wider than
the thorax, very little narrowed at apex, surface finely striate, striæ finely
punctured, intervals flat, the third and fifth with three or four fine, sometimes
scarcely visible punctures situated near the second and fourth striæ. Body
beneath with very sparse punctures and very little pubescence. Length .20—
.24 inch; 5—6 mm. (Pl. V, fig. 7).

The males have the first three joints of the anterior and the first
two of the middle tarsi dilated, the latter slightly.

This species exhibits some variations in the lustre of the surface and
in its sculpture, some being quite opaque, others moderately shining, the
latter have the striæ and punctures more evident and the punctuation of
the thorax better marked. I believe they constitute but one species.

As the preceding species shows a resemblance to Nebria so this
resembles *Calathus ruficollis* in smaller size, which has also punctures
on the third elytral interval as fine as in this species.

Occurs in Oregon, Washington Territory, western Nevada and
northern California.

AGYRTES Fröhl.

Head oval not constricted behind the eyes, the latter round and moderately
prominent. Labrum short, transverse, broadly emarginate. Maxillary palpi
moderate in length, first joint very short, second obconical, slightly arcuate,
third short, stout, fourth ovate. Antennæ moderately short, attaining the hind
angles of the thorax, inserted under a feeble frontal margin, first joint robust,
cylindrical, suddenly constricted at base, second and third obconical, the latter
a little longer and more slender. 4—6 short moniliform, the last five forming
a loose club, the eleventh broadly oval. Anterior coxal cavities partly closed
by a slender prolongation of the epimera. Middle coxæ narrowly separated.
Posterior coxæ contiguous. Elytra very narrowly margined, their epipleuræ
narrow. Legs rather short, tibiæ spinulose externally. Tarsi slender. Form
oblong, parallel, body winged.

This genus as noticed by Lacordaire seems to make the lead towards
the Anisotomini. One species only is known in our fauna.

A. longulus Lec. (*Necrophilus*).—Oblong, black or piceous, shining, glabrous. Head coarsely punctate. Thorax one-third wider than long, narrower
in front, sides feebly arcuate from the base, margin not explanate, apex very
feebly emarginate, the angles obtuse, base feebly arcuate, angles obtuse, disc
moderately convex, surface sparsely punctate, punctures a little denser toward
the sides. Elytra a little wider than the thorax, nearly twice as long as wide,
sides very nearly parallel, feebly arcuate, surface moderately deeply striate,
striæ finely crenately punctured. Body beneath rather coarsely not densely
punctured. Femora sparsely punctate. Length .12—.20 inch; 3—5 mm.
(Pl. V, fig. 9).

The anterior tarsi of the male have the first two joints feebly dilated.

Occurs from northern California to Vancouver, rare.

SPHÆRITES Duft.

Head oval, not narrowed behind the eyes but narrowed in front and slightly prolonged. Eyes round, not prominent. Labrum broadly emarginate. Antennæ short, barely attaining the middle of the thorax, subgeniculate, free at base, no frontal margin, first joint rather short, thick, slightly arcuate, second ovate, third slender a little longer than the second, 4—8 small, gradually broader, 9—11 forming an abrupt, pubescent mass. Last joint of maxillary palpi oblong, equal to the two preceding together. Anterior coxæ with large trochantin, the cavities open behind, partially enclosed by a slender prolongation of the epimera. Middle coxæ moderately separated, posterior coxæ contiguous. Legs moderate in length, the tibiæ finely spinulose on the outer edge, the spurs moderate. Tarsi slender, joints 1—4 gradually decreasing in length, fifth as long as the preceding three. Thorax emarginate in front, bisinuate at base, fitting against the base of the elytra, the latter truncate at tip exposing the pygidium. Abdomen of five segments, the fifth a little longer. Body winged.

This genus has so completely the characters of the present tribe that I do not feel warranted in separating it on the number of the abdominal segments, more particularly as the sixth segment shows a marked tendency to disappear gradually as we follow the genera from *Necrophorus* to *Agyrtes*. *Sphærites* combines the peculiarities of *Necrophorus* and *Agyrtes* completing the circle of the table. It has Histeride resemblances but there is no closer relationship.

S. glabratus Fab. (*Hister*).—Form nearly square or slightly oblong, piceous, surface with æneous or bluish lustre. Head sparsely punctate. Thorax twice as wide as long, sides gradually arcuately narrowing to the front, apex emarginate, base broadly lobed at middle, hind angles rectangular, disc very sparsely finely punctulate, sides more distinctly punctured with a moderately deep marginal stria. Elytra as wide as the thorax, very little longer than wide, sides feebly arcuate, apices truncate, disc moderately convex with nine rows of moderate punctures. Pygidium with coarse and fine punctures intermixed. Body beneath black, sparsely punctate. Length .18—.22 inch; 4.5—5.5 mm. (Pl. V, fig. 10).

In the male the middle tibiæ are more arcuate than the female, and the posterior trochanter slightly prolonged and spiniform.

This species occurs in northern Europe, and in our own country from Alaska to California.

Tribe II.—*Lyrosomini.*

Anterior coxæ conical, prominent, contiguous, with a large trochantin, the cavities strongly angulate externally and open behind. Middle coxæ narrowly separated, posterior coxæ separated by an intercoxal process of the abdomen. Abdomen with five segments. Antennæ inserted under a frontal margin, eyes not prominent.

This tribe is distinguished from the Silphini by the separation of the posterior coxæ and from all except *Sphærites* by the abdomen with five segments. It seems to occupy an intermediate position between the Silphini and the elongate Cholevini. One genus only is known.

LYROSOMA Mann.

Head oval, prominent, slightly narrowed behind the eyes which are round, not large and very feebly convex. Labrum deeply emarginate. Maxillary palpi moderately long, first joint very small, second moderately elongate, gradually stouter to tip, third much shorter, fourth nearly as long as second, cylindrical, slightly flattened and obtuse at tip. Antennæ slender, half as long as the body, second joint shorter than the third, joints 3—8 gradually shorter, 9—11 a little broader, the eleventh longer than the tenth, oval, acute at tip. Legs slender. Tibiæ not spinulose externally, spurs slender not long, tarsal claws slender and moderately long. Form elongate, recalling *Atranus*, body apterous.

L. opacum Mann.—Elongate, brownish or piceous, subopaque, surface glabrous. Head sparsely punctate. Thorax subcordate, as broad as long, apex and base equal, sides strongly arcuate in front, sinuate posteriorly, hind angles acutely rectangular, disc feebly convex, a slight impression within the hind angles and an obsolete median line, surface rather irregularly moderately densely punctate. Elytra oblong-oval, deeply striate, striæ punctured, intervals convex. Body beneath not densely punctate, with very indistinct pubescence. Legs paler. Length .28—.30 inch; 7—7.5 mm. (Pl. V. fig. 11).

In the males the anterior and middle tarsi have the first three joints dilated, more broadly in the former, the posterior tarsi are slender and long in both sexes, with the first joint not longer than the second. In the female the anterior and middle tarsi although not dilated are somewhat broader than the posterior.

Occurs in Alaska.

Tribe III.—*Pinodytini.*

Anterior coxæ transverse, feebly prominent, contiguous, with large trochantin, the cavities strongly angulate externally and narrowly open behind. Middle coxæ oblique, not prominent, moderately separated, the mesosternum flat and with an obtuse carina which extends also to the metasternum. Posterior coxæ not prominent, separated by a distinct intercoxal process, oval at tip. Abdomen with six segments, the sixth feebly visible, the first moderately long. Antennæ inserted under a frontal margin. Eyes entirely absent.

This tribe has been instituted for the reception of a small insect which refuses by its organization to enter any of the tribes as at present constituted. The form is nearly that of a depressed *Ptomaphagus*, the head and antennæ rather Anisotomide. The anterior coxæ are very feebly prominent as in many Anisotomidæ, the trochantin is large and finally the cavities are open behind. It seems, therefore, from its entire organization, to be an osculant tribe with affinities equally strong in the direction of the Silphini, Anisotomini or Cholevini.

PINODYTES n. g.

Head short, oval, not prominent, not narrowed behind, eyes entirely wanting. Front margined at the sides. Labrum short, transverse, truncate. Mandibles feebly prominent. Maxillary palpi of moderate length, stout, first joint very short, second obconical, third nearly square, fourth as long as the two preceding together, conical, acute at tip. Labial palpi short, last joint cylindrical. Antennæ attaining the hind angles of the thorax, first joint cylindrical, very little stouter than the others, 2—3 similar, elongate-oval, each very little shorter than the first, 4—6 small, round, seventh broader, eighth equal to sixth, 9—10 similar to seventh, eleventh longer, oval at tip. Prosternum in front of coxæ moderately long. Scutellum small, triangular, base of thorax overlapping slightly the elytra. Legs moderately stout, tibiæ, especially the middle, obliquely truncate at tip and spinous at the outer apical angle. Tarsi five-jointed in both sexes, the first four short and nearly equal, the fifth as long as these taken together, claws slender. Epipleuræ rather broad, body apterous.

P. cryptophagoides Mann. (*Catops*).—Oblong-oval, castaneous, shining, glabrous. Head nearly smooth. Thorax one-third wider than long, apex feebly emarginate, base truncate, hind angles rectangular, sides feebly arcuate and slightly narrowing to the front, disc regularly convex, very sparsely minutely punctulate and under high power finely alutaceous. Elytra as wide as the thorax, sides feebly arcuate, gradually narrowed at apical third, disc moderately convex, surface with sparsely placed minute punctures in the basal region showing a tendency to a strial arrangement, apex absolutely smooth. Body beneath very sparsely punctate. Length .08 inch ; 2 mm., varying a little. (Pl. V, fig. 12).

The males have the first three joints of the anterior tarsi moderately dilated, the middle and posterior tarsi slender.

The distribution of this insect is remarkable. Originally discovered in Alaska, (a type from Mannerheim being before me), Mr. Henry Ulke has lately discovered it in moderate numbers near Washington, D. C. It lives in the fine debris of rotting wood, etc,

Tribe IV.—*Cholevini.*

Anterior coxæ cylindric conic, prominent, contiguous, without trochantin, the coxal cavities feebly or not angulate externally and closed behind. Middle and posterior coxæ variable in position, either contiguous or not. Abdomen with six distinct segments except in *Colon* where there are but five. Antennæ free at base, no frontal margin.

The form of the anterior coxæ varies somewhat in the different genera being almost truly cylindrical in *Leptodirus* and decidedly conical in the other genera. The cavities into which the coxæ are received are worthy of special study, being constructed on a plan which I have not observed elsewhere. The base of the coxa is received into a cotyloid depression in the prothorax the only opening into the cavity of the thorax being a foramen of moderate size in the outer portion of the depression, in the usual position of the trochantin. The form of articulation between the coxa and the thorax is very nearly a ball and socket joint. The coxæ are always closed behind more or less widely and in many of the genera by the meeting of the sternal side pieces on the median line, the prosternum not attaining the posterior margin. This is very evident in *Leptodirus* and *Pholeuon* but in the genera in which the closure behind is narrow it is difficult to decide, although it is probable that the prosternum does attain the hind margin of the thorax in them.

The middle coxæ vary, they may be contiguous or separated, in the latter case the mesosternum is often carinate, very obtusely in *Platycholeus*, while in *Adelops* and *Bathyscia* it forms a prominent keel-like lamina as in many Hydrophilidæ.

The metasternum is at most of but moderate length, in a large number of the species very short, in the latter case the wings are entirely wanting and in the former very feebly developed.

The posterior coxæ may be contiguous or separated in the latter case to a variable degree, widely in *Leptodirus*, by a triangular inter-coxal process as in *Platycholeus* and *Pholeuon* or very narrowly as in *Bathyscia*.

The legs are rather slender and in many species, especially those living in caves, long and spider-like. The tarsi are always five-jointed on the posterior and middle legs the anterior being often four-jointed either in one sex as in *Pholeuon* or in both sexes *Oryotus*. The anterior tarsi are more or less dilated in the males and often the middle also, in the latter case the first joint alone is broader, species occur in *Colon* with the tarsi slender in both sexes.

The tibial spurs are always slender and in one genus *Prionochæta* very long and pectinate on their margins, and in the male of *Colon*, those of the anterior tibiæ especially, dentate at the sides. The antennæ are variable and are sufficiently described with the genera, very little can be said in a general way excepting that in those genera without eyes the antennæ are very long and slender, while in those genera with eyes the antennæ are more or less clavate and shorter. The eighth joint is shorter than the seventh or ninth and in most cases also narrower, there being two exceptions only as far as I have seen, the one in *Leptodirus* with slender antennæ, the other in *Colon* with the clavate form.

The genera included in this tribe have been more or less widely separated by authors, by giving what seems undue prominence to certain characters to the exclusion of others, but with the arrangement of the genera here proposed the relationship between them seems quite evident, *Leptodirus* being of course the more aberrant.

From the curious forms of some of the species of this tribe some erroneous speculations have arisen.

The genera of this tribe may be divided in groups in the following manner :

Abdomen with six segments.
> Posterior coxæ distinctly separated but in a variable degree; elytra usually without sutural stria; antennæ slender and long.
>> Head oval, without eyes..Bathysciæ.
>> Head broad, narrowed to a neck behind and with eyes...........Platycholei.
> Posterior coxæ contiguous; elytra with sutural stria usually deeply impressed; antennæ more or less clavate; head suddenly narrowed behind the eyes forming a neck, the occiput elevated in a ridge...... ....Cholevæ.

Abdomen with five segments (often four in ♀).
> Posterior coxæ contiguous; elytra with sutural stria well marked; head oval not narrowed behind, eyes round and moderately prominent, occiput not elevated..Colones.

The above division in groups seems absolutely necessary, not only for greater convenience of study but also from the fact that the genera included in each represent quite distinct types.

The groups are also very naturally interlinked, the second possessing many important characters of the first and third, while the fourth seems to be related to the third through *Camirus* * Sharp.

The first group contains all the eyeless genera, (*Adelops* having eyes), the species living for the most part in caves. As yet our country possesses no members of it.

The genera of the group Bathysciæ are all European and it might seem out of place to discuss them here, but the study of them has proven so interesting that I have thought it profitable to review them, as their occurrence in some of our caves is possible.

Before proceeding with the discussion it is important to note that *Adelops* does not belong to the group. This genus was founded on a species (*hirtus*), from the Mammoth Cave of Kentucky, which must under all circumstances bear the generic name. The European species included in *Adelops* are members of another and probably of two genera, as will be seen further on. *Leptodirus* and *Bathyscia* were the only genera known at the time of the publication of Lacordaire's genera, the second having been improperly suppressed into *Adelops*, *Pholeuon* Hampe, *Oryotus* and *Drimeotus* Miller, were subsequently described without any reference to their relationship to *Leptodirus*.

To Mr. Schaufuss (Stettin Zeitschr. 1861, p. 424, et. seq.), is due the credit of associating them in a group, to which he adds two new genera through a misconception of the characters of *Adelops* and *Bathyscia*.

The following is his table:

A.—Anterior tarsi dissimilar in the sexes, male five- female four-jointed.
  a.—Anterior tarsi slender in both sexes.
    aa.—Scutellum invisible..*Leptoderus.*
    bb.—Scutellum distinct.
      Body elongate, mesosternum strongly carinate..................*Drimeotus.*
      Body oval, mesosternum feebly carinate....................*Quæsticulus.*
  b.—Anterior tarsi of male dilated. Scutellum distinct.
      Body elongate...*Pholeuon.*
      Body oval, convex..*Quæstus.*
B.—Anterior tarsi in both sexes four-jointed.
   Anterior tarsi slender...*Adelops.*
   Anterior tarsi dilated...*Oryotus.*

In order that this table may be understood in the light of remarks made further on, the following criticisms are suggested.

It does not seem a valid procedure to separate as genera groups of species in which the males have the anterior tarsi very feebly dilated on the one hand or more dilated on the other. I would therefore suggest the propriety of uniting Drimeotus with Pholeuon and Quæstus with Quæsticulus. In these last two and Adelops, Schaufuss is entirely in error. Abeille de Perrin informs us that "all the species of Adelops known to him, more than eighty in number, have the anterior tarsi ♂ five-jointed, ♀ four-jointed, except in three species," neither of which is the type of *Bathyscia*. It is therefore evident that the two genera established by Schaufuss belong to the eighty species above mentioned, and as these do contain the typical species of Schiœdte the name *Bathyscia* must be adopted for them, and the name Adelops as used by Schaufuss becomes doubly erroneous and for the species there included Abeille proposes the name *Aphaobius.*

The next contribution of any extent to the knowledge of these genera is contained in a "*Liste générale des Articulés cavernicoles de l'Europe*," by MM. Bedel and Simon, (Journal de Zoologie, Paris, 1875), from which I have been unable to obtain any ideas of the limits of the genera. The paper is a useful list of species and contains in a foot-note an intimation that the genera have need of a revision.

A more important though less extensive contribution, is that of M. E. Abeille de Perrin, entitled "*Notes sur les Leptodirites*," (Bull. Soc. Hist. Nat. Toulouse, 1878). In this I find the important statement that his collection contains "more than eighty species of *Adelops*, all of which have the anterior tarsi of the male five-jointed and in the females four-jointed, excepting *Milleri* and two unnamed species which have four joints in both sexes." The former which undoubtedly contain the typical species of Schiœdte, represent *Bathyscia*, (*Quæstus* and *Quæsticulus* Schauf.), while the latter species he proposes to call by a new name *Aphaobius*,* (*Adelops* ‡ Schauf.). In this paper M. Abeille gives a table of the genera known to him, of which the following is a copy.

> *A.—Elytra with lateral margin convex without reflexed border visible from above.*
>> *B.—Scutellum barely visible, in fact short and extending across the entire base of the thorax.*
>>> *C.—Elytra glabrous*...*Leptodirus.*
>>> *C C.—Elytra pubescent*..*S. G. Propus.*
>> *B B.—Scutellum normal.*
>>> *C.—Elytra of the length of the body. Thorax subcylindrical and constricted........ ....Antrocharis.*
>>> *C C.—Elytra longer than the body. Thorax subdepressed and slightly narrowed in front of base...............................S. G. Diaprysius.*
> *A A.—Elytra more or less acutely margined and the edge visible from above.*
>> *B.—Anterior tarsi ♂ four-jointed...Oryotus.*
>> *B B.—Anterior tarsi ♂ five-jointed.*
>>> *C.—Elytral margin narrow. Penultimate joints of the antennæ suddenly thickened at tip...... ....Pholeuon.*
>>> *C C.—Elytral margin wide. Penultimate joints of the antennæ thickened from base to tip...Drimeotus.*

Two other genera are mentioned in the paper founded on females alone, and which consequently cannot be placed with certainty in the above table. The first is *Cytodromus*† Abeille, which seems to have no characters given by which it differs greatly from Drimeotus. The second is *Spelæochlamys*§ Dieck, for which I find no valid generic characters given. Having never seen either of these genera it would be presumption to hazard an opinion concerning them, and I can only quote from Abeille, "*on peut dire avec M. Bedel, que les genres qui ont été proposés jusqu'ici ont été fort mal caractérisés ; aucune vue d'ensemble n'a présidé à leur établissement.*"

In confirmation of the above quotation it may be stated that all European authors describe (*Adelops*), *Bathyscia* as having the posterior coxæ contiguous. Through the kindness of M. Sallé I have studied the following European species: *Freyeri, Schiœdtei, Bonvouloiri, Aubei, montanus* and *infernus*, which seem to represent the genus fairly, and all of them have the posterior coxæ separated either

---

* Abeille de Perrin, loc. cit. (in separate pamphlet), p. 8.

† *Cytodromus* and *Antrocharis* Abeille de Perrin, loc. cit. p. 11.

§ *Spelæochlamys* Dieck, Heyden's Reise nach Südl. Spanien, 1870, p. 93; (Berl. Zeitschr. Beih.).

by a metasternal prolongation or an intercoxal process of the first abdominal segment.

I do not understand why M. Abeille has omitted *Adelops* (*Bathyscia*), and *Aphaobius* from the above table. They cannot constitute a separate tribe or even group, but should be placed: *Bathyscia* after *Pholenon*, and *Aphaobius* after *Oryotus*, the regularly oval form separating both of the genera from those to which they are otherwise related by their tarsal characters.

The second group PLATYCHOLEI contains but one genus.

PLATYCHOLEUS n. g.

Form oval, depressed. Head suddenly contracted behind the eyes, occipital ridge indicated by a fine line. Eyes small, transverse to the axis of the head. Antennæ attaining the hind margin of the thorax, slender, gradually thickened externally, eighth joint a little narrower and shorter than the ninth. Last joint of maxillary palpi slender, conical, much narrower than the preceding and scarcely half as long, the third joint stout, conical and truncate at apex, second joint slender. Middle coxæ separated by the mesosternum which is obtusely elevated. Posterior coxæ separated by a broadly triangular process of the first abdominal segment. Tarsi slender, the first three joints of the anterior and the first two of the middle dilated in the males; hind tarsi with the first joint longer than the next three together. Tibiæ not spinulose externally, tip with small spurs and fimbriate with unequal spinules.

The mesosternum separates the coxæ rather more widely than in *Ptomophagus* and is not carinate but forms an obtuse ridge. The head is not provided with an occipital ridge, so that it is more deeply retractile, while in all the other genera in which the head is suddenly narrowed behind the eyes, the occipital ridge is received against the apical margin of the thorax.

P. leptinoides Crotch, (*Ptomaphagus*).—Rather broadly oval, wider in front, depressed, testaceous, moderately shining, sparsely clothed with short luteous pubescence. Head very sparsely and finely punctulate. Thorax more than twice as wide as long, wider than the elytra, apex emarginate, sides strongly arcuate, broadest a little in front of base, rapidly arcuately narrowing to apex, base broadly emarginate, hind angles rectangular, surface shining, very sparsely punctulate. Elytra narrower than the thorax, humeri oblique, sides arcuately narrowing to tip, surface moderately densely punctate, sutural stria wanting. Body beneath sparsely punctate. Length .12 inch; 3 mm. (Pl. VI, fig. 2).

This species has considerable resemblance in facies to *Leptinus*. It is totally unlike any of the species of the tribe. In both sexes the middle tibiæ are arcuate, in the males the anterior tibiæ are broader at apical half, recalling the form of the tibiæ in certain *Stelidota*.

Occurs in northeastern California and western Nevada.

The third group CHOLEVÆ as already remarked contains only genera with eyes, although these organs are feeble in *Adelops*. The head is suddenly narrowed to a neck, the eyes occupying the prominent lateral angle of the head. The tarsi are five-jointed on all the legs in both sexes. The genera all of which are represented in our fauna are as follows:

Mesosternum not carinate, the middle coxæ contiguous, last joint of the maxillary palpi as long as the preceding.
  Antennæ serrate; tibial spurs moderate in length, simple...**Catoptrichus.**
  Antennæ gradually clavate.
    Tibial spurs not long, simple..**Choleva.**
    Tibial spurs very long, bipectinate..............................**Prionochæta.**
Mesosternum carinate, coxæ separated; last joint of maxillary palpi short, subulate.
  Antennæ gradually clavate not longer than the head and thorax; eyes well developed; mesosternal carina at most moderately prominent.
                                       Ptomaphagus.
  Antennæ slender, longer than the head and thorax; eyes small, mesosternal carina prominent, keel-like......................................**Adelops.**

As far as known to me *Catoptrichus, Prionochæta* and *Adelops* are peculiar to our fauna, the others occur also in Europe.

CATOPTRICHUS Murr.

Form moderately elongate. Head suddenly narrowed behind the eyes, occiput elevated. Eyes flattened posteriorly. Antennæ a little longer than the head and thorax, joints 5—10 perfoliate and emarginate beneath as in *Prionus*, the eighth joint one-half as long as either the seventh or ninth, eleventh joint elongate-oval, acute at tip. Maxillary palpi slender, the terminal joint a little longer and more slender than the preceding, acuminate at tip, third joint feebly conical, second slender. Middle and posterior coxæ contiguous, the mesosternum not carinate. Tarsi slender, anterior tarsi and first joint of middle (feebly) dilated in the male; hind tarsi with first joint as long as the next three. Tibiæ finely spinulose externally, the spurs slender, the inner of the posterior tibiæ half the length of the first tarsal joint.

This genus is most closely related to *Choleva* as defined in the present paper and differs only in the structure of the antennæ. It may be hardly necessary to state that this insect was unknown in nature to Mr. Murray and that his remarks are not entirely correct.

One species only is known.

C. Frankenhæuseri Mann. (*Catops*).—Moderately elongate, piceous, elytra, legs and antennæ at base ferruginous. Head moderately densely punctate, feebly shining. Thorax nearly square, angles obtuse, sides very feebly arcuate, the margin posteriorly feebly deplanate, disc posteriorly slightly flattened, surface feebly shining moderately densely punctulate. Elytra ferruginous, oblong-oval, humeri broadly rounded, sides moderately arcuate and behind the middle gradually narrowed to tip, margin very narrowly reflexed, sutural stria moderately impressed, surface substriate, a little more coarsely punctured than the thorax, sparsely clothed with short brownish pubescence and with a faint iridescent surface lustre. Body beneath and legs very finely punctulate. Length .24 inch; 6 mm. (Pl. V, fig. 13).

Male.—Anterior tarsi moderately dilated, anterior tibiæ obliquely excavated and finely pubescent on the inner side near the tip. The tip is furnished with a hook-like process directed from without inwards in addition to the two spurs, reproducing the character found in the posterior tibia of two species of Silpha.

Occurs in Alaska.

CHOLEVA Latr.

Form oblong or oblong-oval, depressed. Head suddenly narrowed behind the eyes, occiput elevated received against the apex of the thorax. Eyes flattened posteriorly. Antennæ as long as the head and thorax, the last five joints forming an elongate club, the eighth shorter and narrower than the seventh and ninth. Last joint of maxillary palpi elongate conical acute at tip, as long as the third joint. Middle and posterior coxæ contiguous, the mesosternum not carinate. Tarsi slender, the anterior dilated in the male, the first joint of middle also stouter but variable in the species. Tibiæ finely spinulose along their outer margins, spurs slender and half the length of the first joint.

By the absence of mesosternal carina this genus is allied to *Catoptrichus* and *Prionochæta*, from the former it differs in the structure of the antennæ and from the latter more especially in the character of the tibial spurs. It is also worthy of mention that while the species of *Ptomaphagus* have strigose elytra, those of *Choleva* with one exception have punctured elytra.

The species are more difficult to separate than those of *Ptomaphagus*, the following table which is necessarily full presents the differences between them. The sexual characters of each species are given as these materially assist in their separation in doubtful cases.

Hind angles of thorax rounded or obtuse.
 Elytra simply punctate.
  Thorax very distinctly narrower than the elytra, not narrowed in front, sides very feebly arcuate.
   Anterior tibiæ of male distinctly sinuate within; abdomen of female without impressions. ....**egena** n. sp.
  Thorax not narrower than the elytra, sides arcuate and narrowed to the front.
   Anterior femora more or less flat on the under edge, usually glabrous and with a tubercle in the male.
    Form oblong.
     Male with the anterior tarsi broadly dilated, the first joint of middle tarsus much thickened......................**luridipennis** ♂ Mann.
     Female with ventral segments 3—6 foveate at middle.
                luridipennis ♀ Mann.

Form oblong-oval.

Male with anterior tarsi moderately dilated, the first joint of middle
tarsus not much thickened...........................**simplex** ♂ Say.

Female with ventral segments not foveate...........**simplex** ♀ Say.

Anterior femora with the lower edge rounded, punctate and without
trace of tubercle in male.

Form oblong, body distinctly coarctate at base of elytra.

Male with anterior tibiæ with a slight sinuation within the tarsi
moderately dilated, the first joint of middle tarsus slightly thick-
ened...**basillaris** ♂ Say.

Female with ventral segments 5—6 rather deeply longitudinally
impressed at middle...**basillaris** ♀ Say.

Form oval, margins of thorax and elytra nearly continuous.

Male anterior tibiæ simple, the tarsi moderately dilated, first joint
of middle tarsus slightly thickened.............**clavicornis** ♂ Lec.

Female with ventral segments 5—6 vaguely impressed.

clavicornis ♀ Lec.

Elytra very distinctly, transversely, finely strigose.

Male anterior tibiæ simple, the tarsi moderately dilated, the first
joint of middle tarsus slightly thickened......**decipiens** ♂ n. sp.

Female with ventral segments simple..............**decipiens** ♀ n. sp.

Hind angles of thorax rectangular, the thoracic and elytral margins continuous.

Male anterior tibiæ stouter, rather suddenly narrowed at base, the
tarsi moderately dilated, first joint of middle tarsus thick.

terminans ♂ Lec.

Female with abdomen not impressed.................**terminans** ♀ Lec.

C. egena n. sp.—Oblong, narrower in front, piceous, elytra luteous becoming piceous from the middle to tip, surface pubescent. Head moderately
densely punctate. Antennæ piceous, two or three basal joints pale. Thorax
about one-fourth wider than long, not narrowed in front, sides very little
arcuate, anterior angles rounded, hind angles obtuse, base feebly arcuate,
surface moderately densely punctate. Elytra oblong-oval, wider than the
thorax, somewhat more attenuate posteriorly, sutural stria moderately deeply
impressed, surface faintly substriate, moderately densely punctate. Body
beneath moderately densely punctulate. Legs piceous, tibiæ and tarsi usually
paler. Length .14—.16 inch; 3.5—4 mm.

In both sexes the lower edge of the anterior femora is rounded.
In the male the anterior tibiæ are distinctly sinuate on the inner
side at middle, the anterior tarsus and the first joint of the middle
rather feebly dilated. The last two segments of the abdomen are
simple in both sexes, without grooves or impressions.

This species might be mistaken for *basillaris* Say, but the narrower thorax together with the sexual characters will serve to distinguish it.

Occurs in Alaska.

C. luridipennis Mann. (*Catops*).—Oblong-elongate, piceous, elytra brownish, surface pubescent. Head rather coarsely and moderately densely punctate.
Antennæ piceous, basal half pale. Thorax more than half wider than long,

narrower in front, sides arcuate, apical and basal angles rounded, base feebly
arcuate, surface densely punctured, feebly shining. Elytra very little wider
than the base of the thorax, oblong-oval, narrower behind, sutural stria moderately deeply impressed, surface without trace of striæ, moderately closely punctate. Body beneath finely punctate. Legs piceous or brownish. Length .16—
.18 inch; 4—4.5 mm. (Pl. V, fig. 17).

In both sexes the anterior femora are flattened on the under
edge and feebly punctate, the male has usually a small tubercle
also at the middle, but this does not seem constant or at least
very evident in all specimens. The anterior tibiæ in both sexes
are simple. In the male the anterior tarsi are rather broadly
dilated and the first joint of the middle twice as stout as the
second. In the female the ventral segments 3—6 are foveate at
middle, vaguely in the first two, more distinctly in the last two
segments.

This species has almost exactly the form of *basillaris* as well as
the color, but is known by the form of the femora and the sexual
characters. Specimens occur with the elytra darker in color with the
surface having a fuliginous lustre.

Occurs from Alaska to Oregon, and New England States.

C. simplex Say, (*Catops*).—Oval, slightly oblong, piceous or brownish,
elytra very little paler, surface pubescent. Head moderately densely punctate.
Antennæ piceous, two basal joints paler. Thorax about one-half wider than
long, a little narrowed in front, sides moderately arcuate, anterior angles
rounded, basal angles obtuse, base feebly arcuate, surface densely and rather
finely punctate. Elytra scarcely wider than the thorax, more narrowed behind,
sutural stria moderately impressed, surface not striate, moderately densely
punctate. Body beneath and legs moderately densely punctate. Length .14—
.16 inch; 3.5—4 mm.

The anterior femora are distinctly flattened beneath and in the
male with a distinct tubercle at middle. The anterior tarsi of
the male are moderately dilated and the first joint of the middle tarsus distinctly thickened. The anterior tibiæ are simple in
both sexes, not sinuate. The ventral segments are simple in both
sexes.

This species is less elongate than *luridipennis* and more nearly
resembles in form *clavicornis*.

Widely distributed in the central portion of the Atlantic region.

C. basillaris Say, (*Catops*).—Oblong moderately elongate, piceous, elytra
paler at base piceous at apex, surface pubescent, moderately shining. Head
moderately densely punctate. Antennæ piceous, two or three basal joints
paler. Thorax more than half as wide as long, slightly narrowed in front,
sides moderately arcuate, anterior angles rounded, basal angles obtuse, base

feebly arcuate, surface moderately shining not densely punctate. Elytra very little wider than the thorax, narrower behind, sutural stria feebly impressed, surface rather shining, not densely punctate. Body beneath moderately densely punctulate. Length .12—.16 inch; 3—4 mm.

The anterior femora beneath are rounded, not flattened, without trace of tubercle. In the male the anterior tarsi are moderately dilated and the first joint of the middle evidently thickened. The anterior tibiæ male have a slight sinuation within. In the females the fifth and sixth ventral segments are rather deeply longitudinally impressed at middle.

This species, the *Spenciana* of our lists, is so plainly the species intended by Say, that I have no hesitation in using his name. Murray has already indicated the synonymy of *cadaverinus* Mann., and I find *brunnipennis* Mann. not differing. Types of the last two are before me.

This is the most widely distributed species known to me. It extends from Alaska to California and Nevada to the Lake Superior region, White Mountains and as far south as the Middle States, with some variation in color and lustre.

C. clavicornis Lec. (*Catops*).—Oval slightly oblong, brownish-piceous, elytra sometimes paler, pubescent. Head moderately coarsely not densely punctate. Antennæ a little shorter than usual, scarcely attaining the hind angles of the thorax, piceous, apical and two basal joints paler. Thorax twice as wide as long, narrowed in front, sides rather strongly arcuate, apical angles rounded, the basal obtuse, base feebly arcuate, surface moderately densely punctate with a tendency to the formation of short transverse strigose. Elytra oval, gradually arcuately narrowed to apex, not wider than the thorax, sutural stria finely impressed, surface moderately densely punctate. Body beneath densely punctulate. Femora faintly strigose. Length .10—.12 inch.

The femora beneath are rounded and not flattened. The anterior tibiæ of the male are not sinuate within the tarsi moderately dilated. The first joint of the middle tarsus is also moderately thickened. In the female the fifth and sixth ventral segments at middle have a feeble longitudinal impression.

This species has been improperly placed as a synonym of *brunnipennis* = *basillaris* but it is very distinct. In outline it has the margins of the thorax and elytra almost continuous, the antennæ are shorter and finally the sexual characters differ.

Occurs from Michigan to Texas, Middle States to Colorado.

C. decipiens n. sp.—Oblong-oval, brownish, pubescent. Head finely sparsely punctulate. Antennæ piceous, pale at base. Thorax a little less than twice as wide as long, narrowed in front, sides arcuate, apical and basal angles rounded, the former, however, more distinct, base broadly arcuate, surface finely not densely punctulate, with feeble strigosity near the margin. Elytra not wider than the thorax, about one and a half times longer than wide, sides feebly arcuate and gradually narrowed to apex, sutural stria moderately impressed, disc obsoletely substriate, surface very finely and densely transversely strigose. Body beneath and femora moderately densely punctulate. Length .14 inch; 3.5 mm.

The lower edge of the femora is acute near the base, slightly grooved and smooth externally. The anterior tibiæ of the male are simple, not sinuate, the tarsi moderately dilated, the first joint of middle tarsi moderately thickened. The ventral segments are simple in both sexes.

This species has some resemblance to *Ptom. nevadicus* as well as to *luridipennis* of the present genus, but it is readily recognized by its strigose elytra, a character otherwise unknown in the genus.

Occurs at Olympia, Washington Territory, (Morrison).

C. terminans Lec. (*Catops*).—Oblong-oval, piceous or brownish, pubescent, margins of thorax and elytra continuous. Head moderately densely punctulate. Antennæ piceous, apical and two basal joints paler. Thorax twice as wide at base as long, sides arcuate and narrowed to the front, apical angles obtuse, basal angles rectangular but not produced, base truncate, surface densely finely punctulate. Elytra as wide at base as the thorax, gradually arcuately narrowing to the apex, sutural stria moderately deeply impressed, surface not very densely punctate. Body beneath moderately densely punctulate. Length .10—.12 inch; 2.5—3 mm.

The lower edge of the anterior femora is flat and curved in its entire length without trace of tubercle in the male. The males have the anterior tibiæ stouter than in the female and more suddenly narrowed at base, the tarsi are also moderately dilated, the first joint of middle tarsi proportionately stouter than in any other species. The abdomen is not impressed in either sex.

The form of the hind angles is peculiar to this species in the present genus and a relationship to *Ptomaphagus* indicated.

Occurs from Canada to Massachusetts, Virginia and Illinois.

PRIONOCILÆTA n. g.

Form elongate-oval, moderately convex. Head suddenly narrowed behind the eyes, occiput elevated received against the apex of the thorax. Eyes oval, flattened posteriorly. Antennæ as long as the head and thorax, feebly thickened externally, last four joints rather abruptly shorter than the preceding, the eighth shorter and very little narrower than the ninth. Last joint of maxillary palpi elongate conical, acute at tip, equal to the third joint. Middle coxæ contiguous, mesosternum flat. Hind coxæ contiguous. Tarsi slender, the anterior dilated in the male, first joint of the posterior nearly equal to the others united. Spurs of middle and hind tibiæ long, the inner nearly equal to the first joint of the tarsi, the spurs of all the tibiæ pectinate on both margins with fine spinules. Anterior tibiæ with two spinules at outer apical angle, the middle and posterior finely spinulose along the entire margin, the tip fimbriate with closely placed spinules of unequal length.

This genus represented only by *Catops opacus* Say, is allied to *Choleva*, but differs in the structure of the antennæ, the tibial spurs and the absence of dilatation in the middle tarsi of the male.

P. opaca Say, (*Catops*).—Oblong-oval, a little narrower posteriorly, thoracic and elytral margins very nearly continuous, black feebly shining, clothed with short dark brown hair. Head finely and densely punctured. Antennæ attaining the hind angles of the thorax, piceous, apical and two basal joints pale. Thorax less than twice as wide as long, narrowed in front, apical angles broadly rounded, apex truncate. sides broadly arcuate, at base slightly narrower, hind angles obtuse, base slightly arcuate, surface densely and finely punctulate. Elytra as wide as the thorax, a little more than twice as long as it, sides moderately arcuate and gradually narrowed toward the tips which are more obtuse in the male than in the female, the latter has the sutural angle very slightly prominent, surface moderately densely punctulate, substriate near the tip, the sutural stria well marked. Body beneath and legs moderately densely punctulate, the femora slightly strigose. Length .20 inch; 5 mm. (Pl. V, fig. 14).

Occurs in the northern States from Canada to Pennsylvania and Ohio, not common.

PTOMAPHAGUS Illig.

Form oval or slightly oblong or cuneiform. Head suddenly narrowed behind the eyes, occiput with a ridge received against the apex of the thorax. Eyes flattened posteriorly. Antennæ nearly as long as the head and thorax, gradually clavate, eighth joint always shorter and often a little narrower than the seventh and ninth. Maxillary palpi with last joint short, subulate, third elongate-oval truncate at tip, second slender. Middle coxæ separated by the mesosternum which is moderately strongly carinate. Posterior coxæ contiguous. Tarsi slender the anterior alone dilated in the male, the middle and posterior with the first joint as long or a little longer than the next two. Tibiæ finely spinulose externally, the spurs slender but not long.

This genus has been alternately suppressed and revived by authors who have treated this family more or less completely, but the characters separating it from the surrounding genera are so well marked and the facies of the species so decided that it seems as well founded as any of the genera of the tribe. It does not seem, however, that *Catopomorphus* is sufficiently distinct from the present, the trifling difference in the size of the eighth joint of the antenna hardly suffices to separate it generically.

The species of this genus all have the elytra and often the thorax also strigose, a character not elsewhere found well marked in our species of this tribe except in *Adelops*. Both sides of the continent furnish representatives of the genus, the greater number are however eastern.

The genus as defined by the table of species is composed of quite homogeneous material. Several points of difference have been observed between groups of species which appear to have escaped observation. The antennal character is well known and needs no further comment. The point of next importance in the table is the character of the thoracic sculpture accompanied by one of still more utility in this family and elsewhere—the fimbriation of the tips of the middle and posterior tibiæ. Where the thorax is distinctly strigose the tibiæ are fimbriate with short, closely placed equal spinules, and in those with the thorax simply punctured the spinules are unequal. It might be noticed here that in genera, even those not remotely related, in which there is a resemblance more or less great in general appearance, there is a tendency to repeat or reproduce special characters. Among these instances I might cite *Conosoma, Ptomaphagus, Eucinetus, Eustrophus* and *Mordella*, in which the tibiæ are fimbriate with short equal spinules. Other more minute resemblances occur in these genera but this is not the place for their exposition, and with this hint for the benefit of others I will defer the further consideration to the future in a separate essay.

The other characters in the table need no special comment and the table is now presented as a condensation of the important characters of each species.

Eighth joint of antennæ very short and transverse, somewhat narrower than the seventh or ninth.

    Thorax transversely strigose; middle and posterior tibiæ fimbriate with short, equal, closely placed spinules.

        Strigæ of elytra not very closely placed, surface moderately shining.

            Elytra very obliquely strigose.............................**consobrinus** Lec.

            Elytra transversely strigose.....................................**californicus** Lec.

        Strigæ of elytra very densely placed, transverse. Subopaque.

                                        nevadicus n. sp.

    Thorax punctate, rarely strigose near the margin; middle and posterior tibiæ fimbriate with unequal spinules.

        Inner spur of posterior tibiæ as long as the first tarsal joint; sutural stria rather feebly impressed...................................**oblitus** Lec.

        Inner spur short, less than half the first joint; sutural stria deeply impressed...**pusio** Lec.

Eighth joint of antennæ at least half the length of the ninth and scarcely narrower.

    Thorax not twice as wide at base as long, elytra oval gradually arcuately narrowing to apex...**parasitus** Lec.

    Thorax more than twice as wide at base as long, elytra conjointly somewhat triangular, rapidly narrowed from base to apex..**brachyderus** Lec.

Of the above species two are peculiar to the Pacific region, one extends across the Continent, the others are confined to the Atlantic region.

Pt. consobrinus Lec. (*Catops*).—Form oblong-oval, somewhat cuneiform or Mordella-like, brownish or piceous, feebly shining, pubescent, legs and antennæ at base paler. Head sparsely punctulate, pubescence radiating. Thorax one-third wider at base than long, slightly narrowed in front, sides feebly arcuate, base slightly arcuate, hind angles acutely rectangular, surface entirely transversely strigose. Elytra gradually narrowing, sides very feebly arcuate, apex suddenly obliquely narrowed, sutural angle not prominent, sutural stria moderately deeply impressed, surface very obliquely strigose. Body beneath moderately densely punctulate, femora strigose. Middle and posterior tibiæ fimbriate at tip with short equal spinules. Length .08—.12 inch; 2—3 mm. (Pl. V, fig. 15).

This species varies a little in color by having the elytra paler than the thorax. Some specimens have the strigosity a little less oblique near the tip but no other differences are observed.

This is our most widely distributed species being found from Michigan to Florida, Texas, Arizona and California, (Owen's Valley). It does not appear to occur in the maritime regions of the Pacific.

Pt. californicus Lec. (*Catops*).—Brownish or piceous, pubescent, closely resembling *consobrinus* but a little more oval, the sides of the elytra more arcuate and the surface *transversely* and more finely strigose. Middle and posterior tibiæ fimbriate with short closely placed equal spinules. Length .10—.12 inch; 2.5—3 mm.

This species is the representative of the preceding in the maritime regions of California, extending from San Diego northward.

Pt. nevadicus n. sp.—Brownish-piceous, subopaque, pubescent, oval, slightly oblong, subdepressed. Head finely punctulate, pubescence radiating. Antennæ piceous, four basal joints and tip paler. Thorax nearly twice as wide at base as long, sides feebly arcuate and gradually narrowed to the front, base slightly sinuate each side, hind angles slightly prolonged, surface very finely and densely strigose. Elytra gradually narrowing, sides very feebly arcuate, tip obliquely subtruncate, sutural stria moderately deeply impressed, surface *very densely and finely* strigose. Body beneath finely punctulate. Femora finely strigose, tibiæ fimbriate at tip with short equal spinules, the inner spur of the posterior tibia a little longer than half the first joint. Length .12 inch; 3 mm.

Abundantly distinct from the two preceding species by its more depressed form and the very dense and fine strigosity of the surface, which requires a moderate power to be seen.

One ♀ specimen from western Nevada, collected by H. K. Morrison.

Pt. oblitus Lec. (*Catops*).—Brownish or piceous, feebly shining, pubescent, form oval, slightly oblong, equally narrowed. Head sparsely punctate. Antennæ piceous, basal joints paler, eighth joint much shorter and narrower than the ninth. Thorax twice as wide as long, feebly narrowed to the front, sides slightly arcuate, base arcuate, hind angles obtuse, surface punctured with

faint tendency to strigosity at the sides. Elytra as wide as the thorax, sides
feebly arcuate, apices obtuse, sutural angle obtuse, sutural stria moderately
impressed, surface transversely strigose, the strigæ not deep nor closely placed,
pubescence rather coarse. Body beneath somewhat paler than above, finely
punctulate, femora finely strigose. Hind tibiæ with rather long spurs, the
inner equalling in length the first joint of the tarsus, fimbriate at tip with
unequal spinules. Length .08 inch; 2 mm.

A small species easily known by the characters in the table, occur-
ing in Georgia and Florida.

Pt. pusio Lec. (*Catops*).—Castaneous or piceous, moderately shining, pubescent. Form of *oblitus* which it resembles in most of its characters and differing in having the hind angles of thorax nearly rectangular, the sutural stria
more deeply impressed and the inner spur of the hind tibiæ not longer than
half the first joint. Length .06—.08 inch; 1.5—2 mm.

I have seen two specimens clearly identical from California and
Vancouver, but I have provisionally placed with them some specimens
from the Michigan and Lake Superior region, which differ in being a
little more shining and with the strigosity of the elytra slightly oblique.
It has been observed in *consobrinus* that similar differences do not
seem to be specific.

Pt. parasitus Lec. (*Catops*).—Piceo-rufous or castaneous, shining, clothed
with fine pubescence, form oval, narrower posteriorly. Head sparsely punctate.
Antennæ with eighth joint not narrower than the ninth and at least half as
long. Thorax a little less than twice as wide at base as long, sides moderately
arcuate and gradually narrowing to the front, hind angles subrectangular, base
very feebly bisinuate, surface moderately densely punctate, slightly strigose
near the sides. Elytra gradually arcuately narrowing from the base, apex
obtuse, sutural angle rounded, sutural stria moderately deeply impressed, surface nearly transversely strigose, the strigæ rather coarse and distant. Body
beneath finely punctate, femora strigose. Tibiæ fimbriate at tip with unequal
spinules, the spurs of the posterior tibiæ short. Length .08 inch; 2 mm.

The antennal character serves to separate this and the next species
from those which precede, but its importance generically seems to
have been exaggerated.

Occurs from New York to District of Columbia, in the nests of a
black ant.

Pt. brachyderus Lec. (*Catops*).—Castaneous, moderately shining, finely
pubescent, form broadly oval rapidly narrowing from the base of the elytra.
Head finely punctate. Antennæ as in *parasitus*. Thorax much more than
twice as wide at base as long, sides arcuate and rapidly narrowing to the front,
base sinuate on each side, hind angles rectangular, slightly prolonged, surface
finely not densely punctulate on the disc and sides. Elytra but little longer
than wide at base, sides feebly arcuate rapidly narrowing posteriorly, apices
subobliquely truncate, sutural stria moderately impressed, surface finely and
closely transversely strigose with a tendency to become simply punctate near
the suture. Body beneath not densely punctulate, femora substrigose. Tibiæ

fimbriate at tip with unequal spinules, the spurs short. Length .10—.12 inch; 2.5—3 mm. (Pl. V, fig. 16).

This species appears to resemble *Catops depressus* Murr. in form, but as he places that in the series with the mesosternum simple there does not appear to be any further relationship.

Occurs from Nova Scotia to New York, very rare.

ADELOPS Tellkampf.

Oval, narrower behind, convex, body above arched. Head suddenly narrowed behind, the angles prominent as in *Ptomaphagus*, occiput elevated, received against the apex of the thorax. Eyes small, normally placed, without pigment. Antennæ slender, a little longer than the head and thorax, the basal joint received in repose in a deep groove at the side of the head, the last five joints forming an elongate loose club, the eighth joint being shorter and a little narrower than the seventh or ninth. Maxillary palpi with the last joint slender, subuliform, third obconical truncate, second slender. Middle coxæ separated, the mesosternum with a strong keel-like carina. Metasternum short, body apterous, posterior coxæ contiguous. Tarsi slender, the anterior dilated in the male, the first joint of posterior equal to the two following. Tibiæ very finely spinulose externally, the spurs small.

The anterior tarsi are five-jointed in both sexes. This genus is very closely allied to *Ptomaphagus* and I am in doubt whether it should be retained as distinct. The only differences are: the small eyes, the deep depression at the side of the head and the very strong mesosternal carina. The antennæ are also longer and more slender. It may be hardly necessary to remark that the European species referred to *Adelops* do not belong there, as they have a narrow head deeply inserted in the thorax and absolutely deprived of eyes. For these the name BATHYSCIA Schiœdte, should be used.

A. hirtus Tellk.—Oval, narrower behind, pale brown, moderately shining, clothed with yellowish brown pubescence. Head finely and sparsely punctulate, pubescence arranged in a radiating manner from the centre of the vertex. Thorax nearly twice as wide as long, sides gradually arcuate narrowing from base to apex, hind angles rectangular, base squarely truncate, surface sparsely punctulate at middle, strigose at the sides. Scutellum short, broad, usually concealed in repose. Elytra a little narrower than the thorax, sides feebly arcuate gradually converging, apex gradually narrowed, sutural angle obtuse ♂, acute ♀, surface rather coarsely strigose, the lines of minute punctures slightly oblique, sutural stria entire deeply impressed. Body beneath very finely punctulate, femora strigose. Length .08—.10 inch; 2—2.5 mm. (Pl. VI, fig. 1).

Occurs in Mammoth Cave, Kentucky, as well as in other caves on the western side of the mountains.

At this point it is proper that the attention of observers should be directed to the collection of the coleoptera in our large caves. It seems hardly probable that but one Silphide should live in them and it not eyeless.

The group COLONES contains but two genera thus far described, one only occurs in our fauna, the other is from Auckland, N. Z., they are distinguished in the following manner :

Antennæ gradually clavate, eighth joint not narrower nor shorter than the contiguous joints; last joint of maxillary palpi slender.......................**Colon.**
Antennæ very slightly thicker externally, eighth joint shorter and a little narrower than the seventh and ninth; last joint of maxillary palpi dilated, subsecuriform................................ ....**Camiarus.**

The genus *Camiarus* presents all the essential features of the tribe Cholevini as defined in the present paper, and must be referred to the present group by the form of the head and the structure of the abdomen. It is however, somewhat of a synthetic type, presenting a structure of antenna more nearly resembling that seen among the first two groups than of the Cholevæ taken collectively. I am not able to perceive the relationship with the Scydmænidæ which Dr. Sharp intimates, although one of the species does certainly resemble a robust Eumicrus in facies. The dissimilarity in form of the two species seems to indicate the occurrence of others. For specimens I am indebted to the great liberality of Dr. Sharp to whom we owe our knowledge of them, (Ent. Mo. Mag. xiii, p. 23). Figures of the two species will be found on Pl. VI, fig. 24—25.

COLON Herbst.

Form oblong-oval, usually moderately convex. Head oval, not narrowed behind the eyes, occiput not elevated. Eyes nearly round, moderately prominent. Antennæ rarely passing the middle of the thorax, first joint moderately stout not long, second nearly as stout but shorter, third more slender than the second and variable in length. joints 4—7 usually short, gradually wider, 8—11 forming an oblong moderately compact club. Last joint of maxillary palpi slender, subulate. Middle coxæ separated, the mesosternum not carinate, posterior coxæ contiguous. Tarsi slender, the middle and posterior usually compressed, and with the first joint somewhat shorter than the second, the anterior usually dilated in the male. Tibiæ spinulose, the spurs in the male broader from middle to base or in the anterior tibia dentate at the sides. Abdomen with five segments, the terminal often retracted and showing but four.

This genus is separated from all others in the tribe by the structure of the antennæ, head and abdomen.

In most if not all of the books the mesosternum is said to be carinate, this is not so in any of our species not even in that which I recognize as *bidentatum.*

The most curious character observed, and one which appears to have escaped notice, is the structure of the tibial spurs in the male. On the anterior tibia especially, the front spur is short and stout and at the sides dentate or lobed, recalling somewhat the structure ob-

served in the *Triplectrus* group of Anisodactylus or the *Triæna* group
of Amara, The larger spur of the middle and posterior tibiæ is
slender but abruptly wider from the middle to the base. This form
of spur is important in the determination of sex, as some species
have the anterior tarsi as slender in the male as in the female, so
that the presence of a permanent character common to all males
enables us at once to determine to which group a species should
be referred.

The importance of sexual differences in the male has always been
recognized as a means of fitly dividing the species in groups, by all
authors who have studied the genus, (Erichson, Kraatz, Tournier and
Thomson), the latter even going so far as to separate those with
anterior tarsi dilated and those not so into two genera.

Recognizing the value of some independent characters for the
determination of sex, one which will be common to all the species
and not to a part only, M. Henri Tournier (Ann. Ent. Soc. Fr. 1863,
p. 134), states that the males have five abdominal segments and the
females but four. He says: "I have been able to convince myself
that this character is constant, I have observed it in nature on all the
species of the genus with the exception of *C. emarginatus* Rosenh.,
which I have not been able to procure."

In a very careful examination of our species I am prepared to say
that this character has absolutely no value as far as they are concerned.
In support of my own assertion the following table is presented which
can be made instructive from another standpoint.

	MALES.		FEMALES.	
	four segments.	five segments.	four segments.	five segments.
1. bidentatum.	0	2	0	0
2. paradoxum.	0	2	0	0
3. dentatum.	0	1	1	0
4. Hubbardi.	0	5	0	0
5. putum.	0	7	0	0
6. celatum.	0	1	0	0
7. magnicolle.	4	3	0	0
8. pusillum.	8	2	1	0
9. inerme.	1	1	1	0
10. thoracicum.	0	1	0	1
11. asperatum.	2	0	1	1
12. clavatum.	4	3	0	0
13. nevadense.	5	1	1	0
	24	29	5	2

From the above list it will be seen that 60 specimens have been observed, 53 ♂ and 7 ♀, with several others too mutilated to be safely made use of. The table shows the relative frequency of the sexes. Of the 53 males 24 have four abdominal segments visible, 29 have five segments. Of the females 5 have four segments and 2 have five. Thus the value of the number of segments in determining the sex of our species is completely disproved by the statistical arrangement of the specimens.

Another point in connection with this is a comparison of the European species with our own on other characters. Of the twenty-four species included in the admirable monograph by Tournier, twenty-two have the posterior thighs of the male variably dentate, one only has simple thighs and of one the male is unknown. In the preceding list of our species five (*bidentatum* is probably introduced and not counted at this time), have dentate thighs and seven simple thighs.

Reverting to the table all the males with dentate thighs have five abdominal segments and the only known female four. The last seven species with the posterior thighs simple, a series in which we greatly exceed the European number, we have ten males with five segments and seventeen with four, and in the females four have four segments and two have five.

From the evidence afforded by our own material it is highly probable that Tournier's statement is entirely correct for the European species and not at all true for those peculiar to our fauna.

The antennal club varies in length and thickness and apparently in the number of joints composing it. In the following pages the club is for the most part called "four-jointed," but in several instances the seventh joint is so much larger than the sixth and approximates more closely in size to the eighth that the club is then called "five-jointed."

The study of the species beyond this point is an extremely difficult one and males only can be determined with certainty even by comparison, fortunately they are more abundant.

The following table will assist the student in the determination of the species:

Anterior tarsi of male slender, not at all dilated. Posterior femora of male toothed near the apex.
   Posterior tibiæ distinctly arcuate, an obtuse tooth near the knee.
                                         bidentatum Sahlb.
   Posterior tibiæ feebly arcuate and slightly narrowed at the knee, without tooth.........**paradoxum** n. sp.

Anterior tarsi of male with three joints rather broadly dilated.
Posterior femora of male toothed.
Tooth of femora long, hind tibiæ arcuate...................**Hubbardi** n. sp.
Tooth short and near the middle of femur. Tibiæ straight.
Form oblong-oval, not broader in front, hind angles of thorax very
obtuse or rounded.
Anterior tibiæ of male sinuate within; punctuation of thorax dense
and conspicuous. Femoral tooth very small...**dentatum** Lec.
Anterior tibiæ of male arcuate; punctuation of thorax rather sparse
and inconspicuous. Femoral tooth very evident...**celatum** n. sp.
Form oval, broader in front, hind angles of thorax distinct almost
rectangular.
Anterior tibiæ of male sinuate within; punctuation of thorax fine
and rather sparse. Femoral tooth small..............**putum** n. sp.
Posterior femora of male without trace of tooth.
Hind angles of thorax distinct, sometimes acutely rectangular.
Body evidently broader in front, the elytra rather rapidly narrowing to
apex with feebly arcuate sides as in *Ptomaphagus.*
Surface subopaque, densely punctured, sutural stria entire; larger
species (.10—.12 inch)...................................**magnicolle** Mann.
Surface rather shining, thorax sparsely punctate, sutural stria evanes-
cent near base, smaller species .06 inch...........**pusillum** n. sp.
Body oblong-oval, not wider in front, elytra behind the humeri usually
wider than the thorax.
Thorax densely punctured with fine equal punctures.
Middle and hind tarsi compressed and distinctly shorter than the
tibiæ, species larger .10—.12 inch...............**clavatum** Mann.
Middle and hind tarsi slender, very nearly as long as the tibiæ,
species smaller .08 inch...................................**inerme** Mann.
Thorax with coarse rather deep punctures with finer ones in the
intervals...**thoracicum** n. sp.
Hind angles of thorax rounded.
Punctuation rather coarse and submuricate, form more convex and more
obtuse in front; color piceous, legs rufous....**asperatum** n. sp.
Punctuation fine, form depressed, oblong; color brown to rufous.
nevadense n. sp.

C. bidentatum Sahlb.—Oblong-oval, a little more obtuse in front, piceous
or castaneous, finely pubescent. Head coarsely punctured. Antennæ attaining
the middle of the thorax, rufous at base, club piceous. Thorax about one-fourth
wider at base than long, sides gradually arcuately narrowing to apex, base
truncate, hind angles obtuse, surface very densely punctate. Elytra as wide at
base as the thorax, sides gradually arcuately narrowing to apex, sutural stria
finely impressed, arcuate at middle, attaining both base and apex, surface very
faintly substriate, densely punctured, similar to the thorax with the punctures
slightly muricate, each bearing a short fine hair. Body beneath densely
punctulate but more finely than above. Femora more sparsely punctate.
Length .10—.12 inch; 2.5—3 mm.
Male.—Anterior tibia slender, straight, squarely truncate at tip, outer edge
extremely finely spinulose, the spurs short, stout, the anterior slightly lobed
at the sides, the tarsus slender, filiform and glabrous. Middle tibiæ straight,

a little broader than the anterior and distinctly spinulose externally, the spurs slightly dilated from middle to base, tarsus distinctly compressed. Posterior femur slightly crenulate along the lower edge and with a small acute tooth near the tip arising from the outer edge, the tibia arcuate and with an obtuse tooth near the base, the spurs slender at tip, rather suddenly broader at basal half, tarsi slightly compressed. (Pl. VI, fig. 10).

Female.—Unknown in nature. The posterior femora are simple, (Tournier).

In this species the antennal club may properly be called four-jointed, the terminal joint rounded or oval at tip. The second and third joints are equal in length the latter a little more slender. I have not made any direct comparison of our specimens with the European species to which this is referred, but I have no doubt of their identity from the excellent figures given by Tournier.

Two ♂ specimens, Massachusetts, (Blanchard), New York, (Ulke).

C. paradoxum n. sp.—Oblong-oval, very little more obtuse in front, piceous, very feebly shining, sparsely pubescent, legs paler. Head densely punctured. Antennæ piceous, paler at base, attaining the middle of the thorax, club four-jointed. Thorax and elytra as in *bidentatum*. Body beneath moderately densely punctulate. Length .08 inch; 2 mm.

Male.—Anterior tibiæ very little broader to the tip, the outer apical angle distinct, the spurs slightly lobed at the sides, the tarsi filiform. Posterior femora with a slight angulation near the apex and obsoletely crenulate at middle, the tibiæ very slightly arcuate and at base a little more rapidly narrowed presenting a slight angle. (Pl. VI, fig. 14).

Female.—Unknown.

This species might readily be mistaken for *bidentatum* or *dentatum* by its superficial characters, the sexual character of the male will distinguish it from either.

Pennsylvania and District of Columbia, (Ulke).

C. Hubbardi n. sp.—Closely resembling *dentatum* in form and color but a little more coarsely pubescent. Thorax and elytra very nearly equally punctate and somewhat more coarsely than in *dentatum*. Antennal club distinctly five-jointed, the seventh joint being also broad. Length .10 inch; 2.5 mm.

Male.—Anterior tibiæ gradually broader to tip, inner margin straight, the outer apical angle slightly acute, spurs as in *dentatum*, tarsi rather broadly dilated. Posterior tibiæ slightly arcuate, the femora with a slender tooth of variable length arising from the inner margin near the tip, the tooth thin but band-like with one of the terminal angles slightly prolonged. Middle and posterior tarsi slightly compressed. (Pl. VI, fig. 13).

Female.—Unknown.

I know of no means by which this species may be distinguished from *dentatum* except by the sexual characters of the male. It is highly probable that the female will have a slight tooth on the femur near the tip. The punctuation here is rather coarser than in *dentatum* and by that means a little experience will enable one to separate them, but this is difficult to communicate by description.

Occurs in Michigan, Tennessee and District of Columbia.

C. dentatum Lec.—Oblong-oval, very little more obtuse in front, piceous to rufous, surface finely pubescent. Head rather coarsely and densely punctured. Antennæ attaining the middle of the thorax, basal joints rufous, club darker, the latter of four joints the terminal narrower and obtuse at tip. Thorax about one-fourth wider at base than long, sides arcuate, gradually narrowing to the front, base truncate, hind angles rounded, surface very densely punctate. Elytra as wide as the thorax at base, arcuately narrowing to the apex, sutural stria finely impressed becoming obsolete near the base, surface densely submuricately punctate, punctures less dense and a little coarser than those of the thorax. Body beneath moderately densely punctulate. Legs more sparsely punctulate. Length .06—.08 inch; 1.5—2 mm.

Male.—Anterior tarsi dilated, the tibiæ broader at tip, slightly sinuate on the inner side, the outer apical angle acute, the spurs slightly lobed at the sides. Posterior femora with a small acute tooth at middle arising from the anterior margin, the tibiæ straight and simple. The spurs of the middle and posterior tibiæ are slightly broader from base to middle, the tarsi slender but slightly compressed. (Pl. VI, fig. 11).

Female.—Tarsi and spurs simple. Posterior femora without tooth. Anterior tibiæ slender. (Cab. Ulke).

On the elytra may be seen very faint traces of striæ near the base, and in the female above-mentioned the sutural stria extends to basal margin but is extremely fine.

Occurs in New York and Pennsylvania.

C. celatum n. sp.—Oblong-oval, not broader in front, subdepressed, ferruginous, feebly shining, sparsely pubescent. Head finely punctulate. Antennæ paler at base, the club darker, the latter four-jointed, the terminal joint longer than the preceding, obtuse at tip and paler. Thorax nearly one-half wider than long, sides moderately arcuate and gradually narrowed to tip, base truncate, hind angles rounded, surface finely but rather sparsely punctulate. Elytra as wide as the thorax, sides moderately arcuate, sutural stria entire but very fine near the base, surface moderately densely punctured, more densely and a little more coarsely than the thorax. Abdomen finely not densely punctulate, sides of metasternum more coarsely punctate. Length .08 inch; 2 mm.

Male.—Anterior tibia rather strongly arcuate, broader at tip, the spurs lobed at the sides, the tarsi dilated. Middle and posterior tibiæ straight, the tarsi slender, slightly compressed. Posterior femur with a triangular acute tooth near the middle arising from the inner edge. (Pl. VI, fig. 12).

Female.—Unknown.

This species resembles *nevadense* of the next series so greatly that it might easily be placed with it without detection except by the male characters. It also resembles *dentatum* in form but is more depressed. This species seems to be our equivalent for the European *Delarouzei*.

One specimen, western Nevada, (Morrison).

C. putum n. sp.—Oval, slightly oblong, evidently broader in front, brownish or ferruginous, moderately shining, finely pubescent. Head rather coarsely, moderately densely punctured. Antennæ pale, attaining the middle of the thorax, club four-jointed, the terminal joint as long as the preceding and obtuse. Thorax one-half wider than long, sides arcuately narrowing to the front, base truncate, hind angles distinct but obtuse, surface moderately shining, finely not densely punctulate. Elytra as wide at base as thorax, sides arcuately narrowing to apex, surface moderately densely submuricately punctate, sutural stria gradually evanescent near the base. Abdomen sparsely punctulate. Metasternum sparsely but more coarsely punctate. Length .08 inch, nearly ; 2 mm.

Male.—Anterior tibiæ gradually broader to tip, the inner edge slightly sinuate, the spur lobed at the sides, the tarsus dilated. Middle and posterior tibiæ straight, their tarsi slender, nearly as long as the tibiæ and slightly compressed. Posterior femur with a very minute tooth at middle arising from the outer edge.

Female.—Unknown.

This species possesses the sexual characters of *dentatum*, but differs in its outward form and the sculpture of the surface. It however reproduces exactly the superficial characters of *pusillum*, but this has no tooth on the femur of the male.

Pennsylvania and District of Columbia.

C. magnicolle Mann.—Oval, slightly oblong, more obtuse in front, piceous opaque, finely pubescent. Head rather shining, moderately densely punctulate. Antennæ passing a little the middle of the thorax, pale brownish, terminal joint oval at tip, as long as the preceding and somewhat paler, club gradually formed, five-jointed. Thorax large, about one-fourth wider than long, a little broader in front of base, sides arcuate and gradually narrowed to the front, base truncate, hind angles rectangular, surface densely punctulate. Elytra a little narrower than the thorax, gradually narrowed toward apex, sides very feebly arcuate, sutural stria entire, surface not more densely punctured than the thorax but a little more roughly. Abdomen very densely punctulate. Length .10—.12 inch; 2—2.5 mm. (Pl. VI, fig. 8).

Male.—Anterior tibiæ gradually broader to tip, the inner margin slightly sinuate, the outer apical angle obliquely truncate, the spurs lobed at the sides, the tarsi rather widely dilated. Middle and posterior tibiæ straight, the tarsi slender, slightly compressed and shorter than the tibiæ. Posterior femur without tooth.

Female.—Unknown.

This species from its form and size can hardly be mistaken for any other. Smaller specimens have a slight resemblance to *clavatus*, but in these the anterior tibiæ of the male are not sinuate within and the outer apical angle not truncate.

Mannerheim describes the posterior angles of the thorax as obtuse but when a distinct view is obtained they are truly rectangular.

Occurs at Alaska, Vancouver, Lake Superior, Michigan and Pennsylvania.

C. pusillum n. sp.—Form, color and sculpture of *putum*, of somewhat smaller size and differing only in the sexual characters of the male.

Male.—Characters of *putum* except that the posterior femora are without tooth.

Female.—Unknown.

There is a specimen from Colorado in the cabinet of Dr. Leconte, differing from the others in having the sutural stria entire, but it agrees so closely in all else that I prefer to refer it here. It seems to be a female and differs from the male in the absence of anterior tarsal dilatation.

Maryland, Virginia, District of Columbia and Colorado.

C. clavatum Mann.—Oblong-oval, equally narrowed at either end, broadest at the middle of the entire length, piceous or brownish, feebly shining, finely pubescent. Head moderately densely punctured. Antennæ slightly passing the middle of the thorax, basal joints rufous, club moderately stout, five-jointed, the terminal obtuse at tip. Thorax about one-fourth wider than long, sides arcuately narrowing to apex, base truncate, hind angles rectangular, surface densely punctulate. Elytra as wide at base as the thorax, sides arcuate and a little broader behind the humeri, sutural stria evanescent near the base, surface not more densely punctured than the thorax but submuricately. Abdomen moderately densely punctate, metasternum more coarsely but sparsely. Length .10—.12 inch; 2.5—3 mm.

Male.—Anterior tibiæ gradually broader to tip, not sinuate within, the tip truncate, the outer apical angle distinct, spurs lobed at the sides, tarsi dilated. Middle tibiæ straight. Posterior tibiæ slightly arcuate, the tarsi compressed, decidedly shorter than the tibia. Posterior femur without tooth.

Female.—Unknown.

This must be classed among our larger species and is known by the sexual characters and form of body.

Occurs in Alaska, Vancouver, California, Nevada and Colorado.

C. inerme Mann.—Oblong-oval, not broader in front, elytra a little wider behind the humeri than the thorax, piceous, feebly shining, finely pubescent. Head rather coarsely, not densely punctate. Antennæ attaining the middle of the thorax, paler at base, club four-jointed, the terminal joint obtuse. Thorax about one-fourth wider than long, sides arcuate, gradually narrowing to the front, base truncate, hind angles rectangular, surface moderately shining, densely punctulate. Elytra as wide at base as the thorax, slightly broader behind the humeri, sides feebly arcuate, sutural stria finely impressed, evanescent near the base, surface a little less densely punctured than the thorax, the punctuation a little rougher. Body beneath moderately densely punctate. Length .08 inch; 2 mm.

Male.—Anterior tibia gradually broader, not sinuate within, the outer apical angle distinct, the spurs lobed at the side, the tarsus dilated. Middle and posterior tibiæ straight, the tarsi rather slender and but little shorter than the tibia. Posterior femur without tooth.

Female.—Anterior tibia slender, the spurs slender, the tarsus filiform. Otherwise as in the male.

Occurs in Alaska, California and Colorado.

C. thoracicum n. sp.—Oblong, moderately elongate, not broader in front, reddish-brown, elytra with a common central cloud, surface slightly shining, sparsely pubescent. Head rather coarsely, moderately densely punctate. Antennæ attaining the middle of the thorax, ferruginous, club darker, four-jointed with the terminal joint obtuse and paler. Thorax one-fourth wider than long, broader in front of base, sides arcuate, hind angles sharply rectangular, surface with coarse, moderately deep simple punctures not densely placed, with finer punctures in the intervals. Elytra a little wider between the humeri than the base of the thorax, broader behind, sides moderately arcuate, sutural stria entire but indistinct near the base, surface with a faint evidence of a strial arrangement of larger punctures near the base and sides, the intervals a little more finely but not very densely punctate. Abdomen moderately densely punctured, metasternum coarsely but sparsely punctate. Length .10 inch; 2.5 mm. (Pl. VI, fig. 7).

Male.—Anterior tibiæ straight, the outer apical angle obliquely truncate, the spurs lobed at the side, the tarsi dilated. Middle and hind tibiæ straight, the tarsi slender, slightly compressed. Posterior femur without tooth.

Female.—The anterior tibiæ are more slender than the male, the outer apical angle obliquely truncate, the spurs slender, the tarsi filiform. Otherwise as in the male.

This species, independently of its sexual characters, is easily known by the base of thorax being evidently narrower than the elytra at base, and the surface punctured after the manner of *Heteroderes*.

Two specimens, one ♂, Missouri; ♀, District of Columbia, (Ulke).

C. asperatum n. sp.—Oblong-oval, broader in front, moderately convex, piceous, slightly shining, legs rufous, surface sparsely coarsely pubescent. Head not densely punctate. Antennæ piceous paler at base, attaining the middle of thorax, club four-jointed the terminal joint longer than the tenth, oval at tip and paler. Thorax one-fourth wider than long, sides feebly arcuate and narrowed to the front, base truncate, hind angles broadly rounded, surface moderately densely submuricately punctured at the base and sides, more sparsely at the middle and front of disc. Elytra a little narrower at base than the thorax, sides feebly arcuate and gradually narrowed to tip, sutural stria moderately deep and entire, surface moderately densely and rather coarsely submuricately punctured, presenting a rough appearance. Abdomen not densely punctured, metasternum at sides coarsely punctured. Length .08 inch; 2 mm.

Male.—Anterior tibiæ gradually broader, the outer apical angle distinct, the spurs lobed at the sides, the tarsi dilated. Middle and posterior tibiæ straight, the tarsi slender and nearly as long as the tibiæ. Posterior femur without tooth.

Female.—Anterior tibiæ more slender, the spurs simple, the tarsi filiform. Otherwise as in the male.

This species is nearly of the form and size of *putum* but is always piceous, the surface more roughly sculptured and the hind angles of thorax more rounded.

Occurs in Michigan, Canada, Illinois and District of Columbia.

C. nevadense n. sp.—Oblong-oval, feebly convex, not broader in front, piceous to ferruginous, finely pubescent. Head rather finely punctured. Antennæ ferruginous, club darker, attaining the middle of the thorax, the club four-jointed, the terminal joint a little larger than the tenth, obtuse at tip and paler. Thorax one-half wider than long, sides moderately arcuate and gradually narrowed to the front, base truncate, hind angles rounded, surface finely and not very densely punctulate. Elytra as wide as the thorax, sides moderately arcuate and gradually narrowed to apex, sutural stria entire, finely impressed, surface moderately densely punctured and a very little more coarsely than the thorax. Abdomen finely but not densely punctulate, metasternum at sides coarsely punctate. Length .06—08 inch; 1.5—2 mm.

Male.—Anterior tibiæ straight very little broader at tip, the spurs lobed at the side, the tarsi slightly dilated. Middle and posterior tibiæ straight, the tarsi slender, slightly compressed. Posterior femora without tooth.

Female.—Anterior tibiæ straight, spurs simple, tarsi filiform. Otherwise as in the male.

This species bears such a very close superficial resemblance to *celatum* before described, that it is impossible to distinguish them except by the male characters which are fortunately very evident.

Occurs in western Nevada, (Morrison).

Tribe V.—*Anisotomini.*

Anterior coxæ conical, prominent, contiguous, with trochantin, the cavities strongly angulate externally and narrowly closed behind. Middle coxæ always separated but in some narrowly. Posterior coxæ contiguous. Abdomen with six segments subequal in length or with the first a little longer, the sixth usually very short. Antennæ variable in the number of the joints either ten or eleven, club variable of 3—4 or five joints; arising under a slight frontal margin in all of the genera.

By a comparison of the above formula with that of the Silphini it will be seen that they differ only in the structure of the prothorax beneath. In all preceding reviews of the tribe the structure of the posterior trochanters has been made use of in a manner which seems entirely false and misleading. I do not find any constant difference between the two tribes in the form of the trochanter, on the contrary there are forms in each which if rigorously interpreted would remove their possessors from the respective tribes. In proof I need only cite Pteroloma of the Silphini and certain Hydnobius in the present tribe. Taking the tribe Silphini as recognized by Lacordaire and his followers, the entire series which I have here separated as Cholevini do not differ materially from the present tribe in the form of the trochanter, but are quite at variance with that found in the larger Silphini.

As a rule any part of an insect which exhibits a decided tendency to vary, not only between species but also in the two sexes, is an extremely unsafe one to use in any system of classification beyond the separation of species.

The separation of the genera of the tribe as found in the books is by no means happy and in some respects apt to seriously mislead. The tables for the greater part either begin with dividing the genera in two series based on the similarity of the tarsi in the two sexes or their dissimilarity, or else the contractile power is taken as the starting point, these systems are sometimes varied by first excluding those genera with five-jointed tarsi on all the feet. It is certainly true that, taken as a whole, those genera with the tarsi similar in the two sexes are not contractile, while those with dissimilar tarsi are contractile, often very much so. Unfortunately we find that both Cyrtusa and Colenis are more contractile than some Liodes or even Agathidium and the character at once fails. The similarity or not of the tarsi in the sexes is a much better means of separation than the other, unfortunately it requires both sexes for positive determination, as a female Colenis is equally well placed in either series if the male is unknown.

The presence or absence of an antennal groove which has done such good service in other parts of the Clavicorn series is here a character of very great value. Reaching its highest development in Agathidium and Liodes, the groove becomes feebler in the other genera but still well marked even in Cyrtusa where a distinct ridge exists within and behind the eye beneath, and the inner limit of the groove is formed by an elevation of the edge of the buccal cavity. Although the existence of the groove has been casually mentioned by various authors, its importance as a means of dividing the genera has not been recognized. By reference to the table it will be found that the genera with similar and dissimilar tarsi in the sexes are rather sharply separated, Cyrtusa being the only exceptional case and this seems to me no detriment to the value of the character inasmuch as it fixes that genus as a very natural link between the two series of genera, a fact which seems admitted by the position in which it is placed.

As in Necrophorus a portion of the clypeus is membranous, so in the present tribe we find a tendency to the same structure. Triarthron has the clypeus entirely membranous, Hydnobius partly so, while in other genera the anterior border is slightly membranous or the entire clypeus may be corneous. The suture between the clypeus and front is rarely well marked, usually entirely obliterated and not visible except the front be slightly translucent.

Of the fifteen genera known in the tribe three only are found outside of Europe and North America (*Stereus* Woll., from Madeira, *Dietta* Sharp, New Zealand, and *Scotocryptus* Girard, Brazil), the remaining twelve are thus distributed: Peculiar to Europe *Agaricophagus* and *Amphicyllis*, peculiar to America *Anogdus*, *Isoplastus* and *Aglyptus*, leaving seven common to the two countries.

The ten genera occurring in our fauna are distributed in the following manner: Peculiar to the Pacific region *Triarthron*, common to the Atlantic and Pacific regions *Hydnobius*, *Anisotoma*, *Liodes* and *Agathidium*, leaving five occurring only in the Atlantic region.

In the following table no mention is made of the contractile power and any sexual difference in the tarsi has secondary mention, this is for reasons already explained. In any cabinet arrangement Liodes should be placed next in front of Agathidium, it is placed in the position it occupies in the table on account of the antennal structure approaching more closely the genera which precede it than those which follow.

A.—Head without antennal grooves.
Posterior tarsi 5-jointed. Mesosternum not carinate.
  Antennal club 3-jointed.
    Tibiæ slender, not strongly spinulose....................**Triarthron.**
    Tibiæ dilated and strongly spinulose.....................**Stereus.**
  Antennal club 5-jointed...**Hydnobius.**
  Antennal club 4-jointed.
    Tarsi 4—5—5. ....**Dietta.**
Posterior tarsi with a less number than five joints. Mesosternum carinate.
  Tarsi with joints 5—5—4 in both sexes.
    Antennal club 4-jointed................................... **Anogdus.**
    Antennal club 5-jointed....................................**Anisotoma.**
  Tarsi 5—4—4 in both sexes.
    Antennal club elongate, loose, 3-jointed....................**Colenis.**
  Tarsi 4—3—3 in both sexes.
    Antennal club 5-jointed....................................**Agaricophagus.**
B.—Head with distinctly limited antennal grooves.
  Antennal club 5-jointed, elongate. Tarsi dissimilar in the sexes...**Liodes.**
  Antennal club 4-jointed.
    Antennæ apparently 10-jointed. Tarsi similar in the sexes......**Cyrtusa.**
    Antennæ distinctly 11-jointed. Tarsi dissimilar ♂ and ♀...**Amphicyllis.**
  Antennal club 3-jointed. Tarsi dissimilar in the sexes.
    Antennæ 10-jointed...**Isoplastus.**
  Antennæ 11-jointed.
    Posterior tarsi 4-jointed in both sexes, the mesosternum not carinate between the coxæ.............................**Agathidium.**
    Posterior tarsi 3-jointed, mesosternum strongly carinate......**Aglyptus.**

The tribe as here constituted is composed of the same genera as in those authors since the time of Lacordaire, he included Clambus

278 GEO. H. HORN, M. D.

which has been very properly removed and with several other genera since indicated constitutes the tribe Clambini.

Of the genera of the second division Aglyptus alone has the mesosternum truly carinate. In some Agathidium the anterior flat portion of the mesosternum is obtusely carinate but not between the coxæ. All the others have a plain mesosternum.

From the characters given by Wollaston it seemed that *Stercus* should be placed near Cyrtusa or Isoplastus, but I am informed by Mr. Charles O. Waterhouse of the British Museum, that the tarsi are actually five-jointed on all the feet in both sexes, and that there is no trace of an antennal groove. It seems however to bear the same relation to Triarthron that *Anisotoma obsoleta* does to the other species. I must here acknowledge the courtesy of Mr. Waterhouse in promptly replying to my inquiries, thereby enabling me, even at a late moment, to insert the present paragraph.

The genus *Dietta* Sharp, (Ent. Mo. Mag. xiii, p. 78), appears to be very closely allied in its more important characters to *Anogdus* Lec., but from the description there are certain characters of such an anomalous nature that a second examination seems necessary. The anterior tarsi are said to be four-jointed, the middle and posterior five. The presence of a less number of joints in the anterior tarsi than in the two following is altogether without parallel in the Anisotomini. The "side piece (epimeron) of the prothorax produced behind the coxæ, but extremely slender, so as to be only a spine—the two not meeting in the middle," is I suspect one of those cases in which the eyes have been deceived, as all the Anisotomini have the anterior coxæ closed behind by the epimera, a fact which is sometimes demonstrable only by the separation of the thorax from the body. The occurrence of only five ventral segments in the Anisotomini is not remarkable as the sixth is often retracted in various genera. The membranaceous clypeus is also observed in Anogdus, Hydnobius and Triarthron, while the antennal structure completely reproduces the former genus. I give place to the genus in the above table on the faith of the characters given by Dr. Sharp, and I have very little doubt that it will prove to be an osculant form between Hydnobius and Anogdus.

At the time p. 224 was written I had entirely overlooked *Dietta* until my attention was called to it by Dr. Sharp. It should therefore be added in its proper place and the numbers changed accordingly.

I am unable to place *Scotocryptus*, the characters given by the author being entirely insufficient, but it seems allied to Aglyptus.

TRIARTHRON Mærkel.

Head quadrangular, front emarginate, clypeus membranous, labrum bilobed, mandibles not prominent, dentate at middle of inner edge, eyes broadly oval, transverse to the axis of the head; beneath without antennal grooves, maxillary palpi with the second joint moderate in length, third short, fourth nearly as long as second, cylindrical, somewhat acuminate at tip. Antennæ nearly as long as the head and thorax, eleven-jointed, first joint short, stout, second half as long, 3—8 gradually shorter and slightly broader, last three joints forming an oblong mass the first two joints of which are broader than long, the last longer, oval and acute at tip. Thorax transverse, feebly emarginate in front. Prosternum short in front of the coxæ, the cavities strongly angulate externally and narrowly closed posteriorly. Middle coxæ slightly separated, the mesosternum oblique, not carinate. Metasternum moderate in length, the side pieces visible. Abdomen with six segments, the last small. Legs moderately robust, femora canaliculate beneath, tibiæ ciliate and feebly spinulose. Tarsi five-jointed in both sexes, joints 1—4 gradually decreasing in length, fifth longer. Tibial spurs stout, moderate in length.

T. Lecontei Horn.—Oblong-oval, ferruginous, moderately shining. Head sparsely punctulate. Thorax twice as wide as long, apex feebly emarginate, base arcuate, sides gradually arcuately narrowing from base to apex, hind angles very obtuse, surface sparsely punctulate. Elytra a little wider than the thorax, humeri obtuse, sides near base nearly straight, gradually narrowed at apical third, disc with eight entire striæ of moderately closely placed punctures, the intervals flat, finely sparsely punctulate, the alternate intervals with distant coarser punctures. Body beneath punctate, sparsely pubescent. Length .12—.14 inch; 3—3.5 mm. (Pl. VI, fig. 15).

Male.—Anterior and middle tarsi with the first four joints moderately dilated. Posterior femora deeply canaliculate at apex, the outer edge serrulate its entire length, the inner edge suddenly emarginate near the base and beyond the emargination with three equal but not large teeth. (Pl. VI, fig. 15 a).

Female.—Tarsi slender. Posterior femora more slender than the male, simple without serrations.

Three specimens seen, two from Oregon and one from the high Sierras east of Visalia, California.

HYDNOBIUS Schmidt.

Head short, eyes round, not prominent, clypeus small feebly emarginate at middle or even slightly membranous. Labrum small usually deeply bilobed, rarely broadly emarginate. Mandibles moderately prominent, toothed at the middle of the inner edge. Maxillary palpi moderate in length, first joint very short, second rather long, obconical, third half the length of the second, fourth nearly as long as the preceding two. Antennæ rarely passing the middle of the thorax, eleven-jointed, first joint obconical, stout, second much shorter but as stout, 3—6 gradually decreasing in length but becoming broader, joints 7—11 forming an abrupt elongate club nearly as long as the rest of the antenna, the eighth joint smaller than the seventh or ninth; antennæ not received in grooves on the under side of the head. Prosternum short in front of the coxæ, the coxæ are conical-transverse, with trochantin, contiguous, the cavities angulate externally and narrowly closed behind. Mesosternum oblique, moderately separating the coxæ, not carinate. Metasternum moderate in length its side

pieces not concealed. Posterior coxæ contiguous. Abdomen with six segments.
Legs moderate, femora stout, tibiæ spinulose externally and with moderate
spurs, stouter in the male. Tarsi five-jointed on all the feet in both sexes,
joints 1—4 gradually decreasing in length, fifth longer.

The only exception to any of the above characters is found in
Matthewsii, in which the third joint of the antenna is longer than
usual and is a little longer than the next two together.

Our species although not numerous seem to equal the entire number
known from other countries, and are readily known by their male
characters. They may be arranged as follows :

Labrum broadly emarginate. Posterior femora not differing in the sexes, the
   male not toothed.
    Third joint of antennæ as long as the next two; intervals of elytra moder-
    ately densely punctate or wrinkled............. .... **Matthewsii** Cr.
    Third joint not as long as the next two; intervals of elytra with a single
    row of fine punctures and finely obliquely strigose...**strigilatus** n. sp.
Labrum deeply bilobed. Posterior femora dissimilar in the sexes, always
   broader and stouter in the male and usually toothed.
   Posterior femur ♂ distinctly toothed.
    Tooth of femur longer than wide, obliquely truncate: punctuation of
    elytra confused.................. ....**longulus** Lec.
    Tooth of femur as broad as long, obliquely truncate; punctuation of elytra
    deep and substriate............... ....**substriatus** Lec.
    Tooth of femur triangular, acute at tip; punctuation of elytra striate
    but feeble.............. ....**latidens** Lec.
   Posterior femur broad, oval, without tooth.
    Punctuation of elytra substriate and coarse....................**obtusus** Lec.

H. Matthewsii Crotch.—Oblong, castaneous or piceo-rufous, shining.
Labrum broadly emarginate. Head sparsely punctate, vertex with slight
impression. Thorax broader than long, somewhat variable in shape, either
slightly narrowed in front or not, apex and base truncate, sides moderately
arcuate, hind angles distinct but obtuse, surface finely punctulate, the punctures
coarser and sparser along the base. Elytra scarcely wider than the thorax,
oblong-oval, with eight entire striæ of fine and closely placed punctures,
sutural stria deeper, intervals flat finely punctulate transversely wrinkled,
the alternate intervals with coarser distant punctures. Body beneath sparsely
punctate, slightly pubescent. Legs paler. Length .14—.24 inch; 3.5—6 mm.
(Pl. VI, fig. 16).

Male.—Anterior and middle tarsi very slightly dilated, the anterior tibiæ
broader and serrulate, the femora stouter than in the female, and the posterior
more deeply canaliculate.

Female.—Tarsi slender. Anterior tibiæ spinulose less dilated than the male.
Tibial spurs, especially those of the anterior tibiæ much smaller.

In several females before me the mandibles have a distinct
tooth on the anterior edge beneath, less developed in the right
mandible. This is however very variable and in one specimen
barely distinct.

It is curious that in this our largest species the sexual characters of the male should be so feeble, all the other species having well marked teeth or dilatations of the posterior femora. The elytral sculpture is also less marked in the male, the punctures of the striæ being always coarser in the female.

Twelve specimens examined from Vancouver and Washington Territory.

Agathidium pallidum Say, may be this species.

II. strigilatus n. sp.—Oblong, pale castaneous, shining. Head very sparsely punctulate, labrum scarcely emarginate. Thorax nearly twice as wide as long, narrowed in front, widest in front of base, apex feebly emarginate, base arcuate, sides arcuate, hind angles distinct but obtuse, surface finely and sparsely punctulate and very minutely strigose, basal marginal line fine, nearly obliterated at middle. Elytra not wider than the thorax, sides moderately arcuate and gradually narrowed from the base, surface with striæ of extremely fine punctures, the intervals flat and finely obliquely strigose, the alternate intervals very distantly finely punctulate. Body beneath very sparsely punctulate. Length .08—.10 inch; 2—2.5 mm.

Male.—Anterior and middle tarsi slightly dilated, anterior femur with a slender spine at the middle beneath. Posterior femur simple. (Pl. VI, fig. 18).

Female.—Tarsi slender. Femora all simple.

By its feebly emarginate labrum, strigose elytra and simple hind femora in both sexes, this species is evidently allied to *Matthewsii*, although widely differing in size and other sexual characters.

Three specimens, two ♂, one ♀, Nevada and Vancouver.

II. longulus Lec.—Form oblong, castaneous, shining. Head sparsely punctate, labrum bilobed. Thorax twice as wide as long, widest at middle, base and apex equal, sides moderately arcuate, apex feebly emarginate, base broadly arcuate, hind angles rounded, disc rather coarsely but not densely punctured, a finely impressed basal line. Elytra a little wider than the thorax, oblong-oval, sutural stria moderately impressed behind the middle and continued to base by punctures, surface coarsely punctate, the punctures moderately dense and with a faint tendency to a strial arrangement. Body beneath sparsely punctate. Length .14 inch; 3.5 mm.

Male.—Anterior and middle tarsi moderately dilated, the posterior femur with a long tooth on the outer side near the knee obliquely truncate at tip. (Pl. VI, fig. 20).

Female.—Tarsi slender, posterior femur more slender than the male and without tooth.

This species has a more coarsely punctured thorax than any other in our fauna, and the sculpture of elytra in addition will serve to distinguish it. The male will be easily separated. With this I unite *longidens* Lec., as I am unable to find any difference.

Occurs in Colorado, California, British Columbia and Oregon, four specimens examined.

II. substriatus Lec.—Oval, slightly oblong, piceous or castaneous, shining. Head sparsely punctate, labrum bilobed. Thorax less than twice as wide as long, narrowed in front, widest in front of base, sides arcuate, hind angles rounded, surface sparsely punctate. Elytra oval, slightly oblong, sides arcuate and gradually narrowed from the base, surface with striæ of moderately coarse closely placed punctures, the sutural stria deeper posteriorly, intervals flat with punctures nearly as coarse as those of the striæ but less regular. Body beneath sparsely punctate. Length .08—.10 inch : 2—2.5 mm.

Male.—Anterior and middle tarsi slightly dilated, posterior femora stout, with a broad tooth near the distal end which is emarginate on the distal edge and obliquely truncate at tip, posterior tibia straight. (Pl. VI, fig. 19).

Female.—Tarsi slender, posterior femora slender without tooth.

Superficially this species resembles *obtusus* and males alone can be distinguished with certainty. With it I have united *curvidens* which does not differ from undoubted males of this species.

Occurs from Nova Scotia to Colorado, through New York, Michigan, and Canada. Nine specimens examined.

II. latidens Lec.—Oblong-oval, brownish or castaneous, shining. Head very sparsely punctate. Thorax nearly twice as wide as long, narrowed in front, widest in front of base, sides arcuate, apex feebly emarginate, base truncate, hind angles distinct but obtuse, surface shining, very sparsely punctate. Elytra oval slightly oblong, sides moderately arcuate, gradually narrowing to base, surface with rows of moderately regular punctures, those of the striæ proper and the intervals equal and often with fine oblique lines connecting the punctures, sutural stria rather deeply impressed and continued by rather deeper punctures to the base. Body beneath very sparsely punctate. Length .06—.08 inch ; 1.5—2 mm.

Male.—Anterior and middle tarsi very little dilated, posterior tibiæ slightly arcuate near its base, the femur stout with a broad triangular tooth, acute at its summit situated near the distal end. (Pl. VI, fig. 21).

Female.—Tarsi simple. Hind femur slender without tooth.

This species differs in its surface sculpture being far less marked and less dense. The sexual characters are quite distinct and seem naturally intermediate between those of *substriatus* and *obtusus*.

Occurs from Anticosti, Canada to Col. and Cal. Four specimens.

II. obtusus Lec.—Oblong-oval, castaneous brown, moderately shining. Head sparsely punctate, labrum bilobed. Thorax twice as wide as long, widest at middle, apex a little narrower than base, the former feebly emarginate, the latter arcuate, hind angles rounded, surface not densely punctate, a fine sub-basal line. Elytra very little wider than the thorax, oblong-oval, sutural stria moderately impressed behind the middle continued by punctures to base, surface with eight striæ of rather coarse punctures, the intervals 2—4—6 with fine punctures closely placed, 3—5—7 with coarse punctures distantly placed. Body beneath sparsely punctate. Length .08—.10 inch ; 2—2.5 mm.

Male.—Anterior and middle tarsi moderately dilated, posterior femur broad and stout, posterior tibiæ arcuate. (Pl. VI, fig. 17).

Female.—Tarsi slender, posterior femur much less dilated, the tibia straight.

This species bears considerable resemblance to *substriatus* and the male characters are the only reliable means of separation.

Occurs in Colorado and British Columbia, four specimens.

ANOGDUS Lec.

Head short, not prolonged in front of the eyes, clypeus short, broadly emarginate, labrum short, feebly emarginate. Mandibles feebly prominent, dentate on the inner margin. Maxillary palpi short, last joint cylindrical slightly acute at tip. Eyes round moderately prominent. Antennæ ten-jointed arising under a slight frontal margin, first joint short, stout, second a little more slender and nearly as long, third less stout and shorter than second, 4—6 short gradually broader, 7—10 forming a very abrupt oblong club a little longer than the preceding joints, 7—8—9 short, transverse, more than twice as wide as long, ten narrower, short, truncate at tip; head beneath without antennal grooves. Prosternum in front of coxæ short, the cavities transverse and closed behind. Mesosternum separating the anterior coxæ, vertical between them and finely carinate. Metasternum rather short, the side pieces narrowly visible, posterior coxæ contiguous. Abdomen with six segments. Legs short, stout, tibiæ spinulose externally. Tarsi slender with joints 5—5—4. Body short, stout, not contractile.

This genus is closely allied to Anisotoma and bears to it the same relation on one side that Cyrtusa does on the other. After a careful manipulation of the unique before me I am unable to find more than ten joints to the antennæ, the eighth joint which is so feebly visible in Cyrtusa appears to be entirely wanting here.

A. capitatus Lec.—Rather broadly oval, brownish, ferruginous, moderately shining. Head rather coarsely punctate. Thorax short transverse, nearly three times as wide as long, slightly narrowed in front, apex emarginate, sides and base arcuate, hind angles broadly rounded, surface rather coarsely punctate, sparsely on the disc, more densely at the sides. Elytra a little wider than the thorax and very little longer than wide, oval, convex, surface with eight rather deeply impressed striæ, the striæ crenately punctured, intervals convex and punctulate. Body beneath and femora sparsely punctate. Length .10 inch; 2.5 mm. (Pl. VI, fig. 22).

The unique specimen, from Florida, before me appears to be a female, its anterior tarsi are however wanting but the femora present no sexual characters. The minute tooth observed on the hind thighs (Proc. Acad. 1866, p. 369), proves to be a deception.

ANISOTOMA Illig.

Head short, not prolonged in front of the eyes, without antennal grooves beneath, clypeus truncate. Labrum small, emarginate or sub-bilobed. Mandibles short robust, simple at tip, dentate at middle (except in *ecarinata*). Eyes round feebly prominent. Antennæ short or moderate in length, eleven-jointed, first joint robust, second nearly as stout but shorter, third more slender and longer (except in *alternata*), 4—6 short gradually broader, 7—11 forming an abrupt oblong club usually as long as the preceding portion of the antennæ, the eighth joint very short and narrower than the seventh or ninth. Last joint of maxillary palpi longer than the third, cylindrical slightly acuminate at tip. Prosternum short in front of the coxæ, the cavities angulate externally and closed behind. Mesosternum moderately separating the middle coxæ and oblique (vertical in *obsoleta*), and variably carinate (not carinate in *ecarinata*). Metasternum moderate in length, the posterior coxæ contiguous. Abdomen with six segments. Legs moderate, rarely long, short and rather stout in *obsoleta*. Tibiæ spinulose externally. Tarsi of moderate length, joints 5—5—4 in both sexes. Body oval or oblong.

As above described Anisotoma is not strictly homogeneous there being two species a little at variance with the others and one of them especially so. *A. obsoleta* has the short robust form of Cyrtusa and a vertical mesosternum between the coxæ although not carinate in the latter genus, here however the divergence from the typical structure ends. On the other hand *A. ecarinata* has the normal oblique mesosternum but there is no trace of carina, further the mandibles are not toothed at the middle of the inner margin. There is however a variability in the degree of carination of the mesosternum among the other species, sometimes the carina is merely a raised line. I have thought it better to admit these exceptional forms in the genus, rather than separate them under names which would probably have but an ephemeral existence.

In number our species are much less than half those of Europe, which fact suggests the possibility that a more careful search would at least double our present number.

The accompanying table will aid in distinguishing those at present known to us. In it I have endeavored to avoid as far as possible the use of sexual characters and have without their aid separated six species, but the other seven have entirely refused to be separated by any other means, and the resemblance is so great in several cases that direct comparison without reference to the male might prove deceptive.

While all parts of our country have furnished specimens, the species appear to have a wide distribution, at least this is shown where a number of specimens have been examined. In several instances one or two specimens only have been accessible and from such a number no deductions can be made. We can however be certain that at least four cross the continent and several others have passed half that extent.

In the table the arrangement seems to show a gradual transition of the species from a resemblance to Hydnobius to a more certain relationship to Cyrtusa.

A. alternata Mels.—Oval, robust, moderately convex, rufo-testaceous or
pale castaneous, moderately shining, legs elongate. Head sparsely punctate.
Antennæ rather short, the club a little longer than the rest of the antenna,
third joint not longer or even a little shorter than the second. Thorax more
than twice as wide as long, a little narrowed in front, apex feebly emarginate,
base arcuate, hind angles distinct but obtuse, surface sparsely punctate. Elytra
a little wider than the thorax, oval, sides moderately arcuate, surface 8-striate,
striæ crenately punctured, intervals slightly convex obsoletely punctulate,
the alternate with coarse, distant punctures. Metasternum alutaceous and
sparsely punctate, abdomen sparsely punctate. Length .14—.16 inch; 3.5—
4 mm. (Pl. VII, fig. 1).

Male.—Anterior tarsi slightly dilated. Posterior legs moderately elongate, the femora not very stout, subangulate or toothed at middle, the tibia slender, arcuate at apical third and somewhat thickened at tip.

Two specimens are before me both males which show some differences, which may with more specimens prove to have specific value.

The first in the cabinet of Dr. Leconte and the type has the eighth stria of punctures entire and without a short subhumeral row of punctures. The posterior femur is merely subangulate at middle. In the second in my cabinet the eighth stria is abbreviated at base and there is a short subhumeral stria. The posterior femora are acutely toothed at middle and the hind tibiæ a little less thickened at tip. The two agree in having the third joint of the antenna short and nearly as thick as the second, while in all the other species the third joint is usually slender and distinctly longer than the second, often much so.

Two specimens, Georgia.

A. humeralis n. sp.—Oblong-oval, moderately convex, piceous, shining, basal margin near the humeri testaceous. Head sparsely punctate, vertex with several much coarser punctures in a transverse series. Antennæ nearly as long as head and thorax, club darker. Thorax twice as wide as long, narrowed in front, sides feebly arcuate, apex slightly emarginate, base arcuate, hind angles rectangular but not prominent, surface sparsely punctate, less distinctly at the sides. Elytra oblong oval, very little wider than the elytra, humeri distinct, surface with eight rows of moderately deep and rather closely placed punctures, the eighth row abbreviated at base and with a subhumeral series of punctures, intervals irregularly bisinuately punctured, the alternate intervals with coarse distant punctures. Metasternum alutaceous with very few punctures, abdomen sparsely obsoletely punctate and alutaceous. Legs piceo-testaceous. Length .16 inch; 4 mm.

Male.—Anterior tarsi moderately, middle tarsi less dilated. Middle and posterior femora stout, the latter with the outer condyle obtusely triangularly prolonged. Tibiæ stout the posterior slightly arcuate. (Pl. VII, fig. 4).

Female.—Tarsi slender. Middle and posterior femora not as broad as the male and without prolonged condyle on the posterior. Tibiæ straight less stout.

I have seen but two specimens, the male in my cabinet, the female with Mr. Ulke. The latter specimen is purely piceous in color with the basal pale space as plainly visible as in my lighter colored specimen. This character seems a good one for readily distinguishing this from any other in our fauna. By the male sexual characters it is related to *conferta* and *obsoleta* but with this the resemblance ceases.

Two specimens, northern California and Oregon.

A. valida n. sp.—Oblong-oval, moderately robust, piceous varying to paler, moderately shining. Head sparsely punctate, vertex with an arcuate row of coarser punctures. Thorax twice as wide as long, a little narrower in front, widest in front of base, apex emarginate, sides and base arcuate, hind angles distinct but obtuse, surface sparsely punctate with a row of coarser punctures along the base. Elytra oblong-oval, a little wider than the thorax, sides moderately arcuate, surface moderately deeply 8-striate, the outer stria abbreviated but rarely with subhumeral stria, striæ rather coarsely creuately punctured, the intervals slightly convex, very finely punctulate, the alternate intervals with coarse punctures distantly placed. Metasternum very finely alutaceous, obsoletely punctate at the sides, abdomen sparsely punctate. Length .14—.24 inch; 3.5—6 mm. (Pl. VII, fig. 2).

Male.—Anterior and middle tarsi very slightly dilated. Posterior femur moderately stout, broadest at middle where it is subangulate or slightly dentate, the lower edge on the outer side slightly crenulate between the middle and the base, the inner condyle slightly prolonged. Posterior tibiæ rather slender, gradually stouter to apex, and strongly arcuate in its entire length. (Pl. VII, fig. 2 a).

Female.—Anterior and middle tarsi long and slender. Posterior femur not stout, the tibia straight and a little shorter than the male.

This species has a resemblance to some of our forms of Phaleria, and in the present genus is somewhat troublesome to distinguish from *assimilis* and the male characters must be relied on. By comparison the two are readily separable.

The distribution of this species is transcontinental on our northern line, extending from the White Mountains (Austin) to Canada, Colorado and Vancouver.

A. assimilis Lec.—Oblong-oval, piceous or rufo-piceous, shining. Head sparsely punctate with an arcuate row of coarser punctures. Thorax twice as wide as long, narrowed in front, apex emarginate, sides arcuate, base truncate, hind angles distinct but obtuse, surface sparsely punctate with coarser punctures at the sides of base. Elytra very little wider than the thorax, oval, a little longer than wide, sides moderately arcuate, surface with eight rows of moderately coarse, closely placed punctures, a distinct subhumeral short row of punctures, intervals slightly convex, obsoletely punctulate, the alternate intervals with coarser distant punctures. Metasternum alutaceous, obsoletely punctate. Abdomen alutaceous, sparsely punctulate. Length .14—.16 inch; 3.5—4 mm.

Male.—Anterior tarsi slightly dilated. Posterior femur not dilated at middle, the lower anterior edge crenulate, the tibia slender, strongly arcuate and flattened on the inner edge. (Pl. VII, fig. 3).

Female.—Tarsi slender. Posterior femur similar to the male but not crenulate, the tibia shorter than the male, stouter and more spinulose.

Closely resembling *valida* this species may be separated by the male characters. It will be observed that the short subhumeral stria is here always present and rather distant from the margin, while in *valida* it is only exceptionally present and not distant from the margin.

Also transcontinental in its distribution, occurring in New Hampshire, Michigan, Canada, Colorado and Vancouver.

A. punctatostriata Kby.—Oval, slightly oblong, convex, shining. Head
sparsely punctate with an arcuate row of coarser punctures. Thorax twice as
wide as long, gradually narrower from base to apex, the latter emarginate, the
base truncate, hind angles rectangular but not prominent, surface sparsely
finely punctate, a few coarser punctures along the base at the sides. Elytra
oval continuing regularly the curve of the sides of the thorax, surface with
eight rows of coarse and closely placed but not crenate punctures, the eighth
abbreviated at base with a moderately long subhumeral row of punctures,
intervals flat, shining, sparsely punctulate, the alternate with distant coarser
punctures. Metasternum finely alutaceous, sparsely punctulate, abdomen shining, very sparsely punctulate. Length .10 inch; 2.5 mm.

Male.—Anterior tarsi slightly dilated. Posterior femora simple beneath,
neither dentate nor crenate, posterior tibiæ straight not differing from the
female.

Female.—Anterior tarsi slender.

This species is peculiar in the almost entire obliteration of sexual
differences, the anterior tarsi ♂ are even feebly dilated but quite distinctly broader than the female. Apart from the sexual characters of the male this species is not readily distinguishable from
assimilis by description. It is however more regularly oval in its
outline, the sides of thorax and elytra being in a continuous curve,
the body more convex and the surface less deeply sculptured and
more shining.

This species follows *assimilis* in its distribution. Synonymous
with it is *læta* Mann., described from Alaska, that described as the
present species is certainly an erroneous determination and is probably
Hydnobius substriatus Lec.

A. difficilis n. sp.—Oblong, rufo-testaceous, shining. Head sparsely punctulate with a few slightly coarser vertical punctures. Thorax twice as wide as
long, narrowed in front, sides feebly arcuate, apex slightly emarginate, base
subtruncate, hind angles obtuse but not rounded, surface sparsely punctulate,
with a few slightly coarser punctures near the basal angles. Elytra oblong-oval,
sides feebly arcuate, surface substriate, striæ with moderate punctures closely
placed, eighth stria much abbreviated, continued by coarser more distant punctures to base, a rather long subhumeral stria, intervals feebly convex very
finely punctulate, the alternate intervals with coarser punctures rather closely
placed. Body beneath finely alutaceous, obsoletely punctulate, the abdomen
more distinctly. Length .12—.14 inch; 3—3.5 mm.

Male.—Anterior and middle tarsi very decidedly dilated. Posterior femora
slightly thickened not serrulate nor dentate, the posterior tibiæ arcuate near
the apex.

Female.—Anterior and middle tarsi more slender and longer than the male.
Posterior femora less stout, the tibiæ shorter, less slender and very slightly
arcuate.

In its general aspect this species resembles *assimilis* but the elytra are more decidedly striate and the form less robust. The punctures of the alternate intervals are also more approximated so that the distance between them is scarcely more than the width of the interval, while the distance is double that in the other species. In its sexual characters it approaches *collaris* but it is a more oblong species than either that or *curvata*.

Two specimens, Owen's Valley, California.

A. collaris Lec.—Regularly oval, slightly oblong, not very convex, piceous to rufous, shining. Head sparsely punctate, vertex with an arcuate row of coarser punctures. Antennal club always darker. Thorax twice as wide as long, narrowed in front, wider at middle than at base, apex emarginate, sides and base arcuate, hind angles obtuse, surface sparsely punctate, a few coarser punctures at sides of base. Elytra oval not much wider than the thorax, sides moderately arcuate, surface with eight striæ of closely placed punctures, the eighth somewhat interrupted at base and with a rather long subhumeral stria which joins the margin, intervals slightly convex very sparsely punctulate, the alternate intervals with coarse distant punctures. Metasternum and abdomen very finely alutaceous and sparsely obsoletely punctulate. Length .08—.12 inch; 2—3 mm.

Male.—Anterior and middle tarsi slightly dilated. Posterior femora rather slender, simple, the tibiæ long and slender, straight at base, arcuate at apical third rather abruptly and somewhat thickened.

Female.—Tarsi slender, posterior tibiæ shorter than in the male and straight. This species may be compared to a diminuative *valida* which it resembles in its form and nearly in sculpture. The sexual characters of the one are a reproduction of the other except as to the form of the femur. As in all the species forming the bulk of the genus the sexual characters of the male afford the only true means of separation.

Occurs in New Hampshire, Canada, Colorado, California and British Columbia, and is a little variable in its elytral sculpture in the various localities, in some the punctures of the striæ are subcrenate.

A. curvata Mann.—Regularly oval, very little oblong, piceous or rufo-piceous, shining. Head nearly smooth, with four coarser vertical punctures. Thorax twice as wide as long, broadest at base, apex slightly narrower, sides and base feebly arcuate, hind angles rectangular but not prominent, surface very obsoletely sparsely punctulate, nearly smooth, a few obsolete larger punctures at sides of base. Elytra regularly oval, not wider than the thorax, surface with eight striæ of not very closely placed punctures, the second and third sinuate, a short subhumeral stria, intervals flat, obsoletely sparsely punctulate, the alternate with coarser distant punctures. Body beneath very finely alutaceous, sparsely obsoletely punctulate. Length .12—.14 inch; 3—3.5 mm.

Male.—Anterior and middle tarsi slightly dilated. Posterior femora slender and simple, the posterior tibiæ long, slender, and regularly arcuate from base to apex and not thickened at tip.

Female.—Tarsi slender, tibiæ straight.

This species closely resembles *collaris* but the thorax is here broadest at base. It is the only species in which I have observed the irregularity of the striæ above mentioned and this seems to have suggested the name. The specimen described by Mannerheim was evidently a female. With it I have united *morula* Lec.

Two specimens, California and Washington Territory.

A. conferta Lec.—Oblong-oval, piceous, elytra paler, moderately shining. Head rather coarsely but sparsely punctate. Thorax a little more than twice as wide as long, narrowed in front, apex emarginate, base truncate, sides feebly arcuate, hind angles distinct but very obtuse, surface sparsely punctate, punctures a little coarser at the sides. Elytra a little wider than the thorax, base at humeri slightly oblique, sides moderately arcuate, sutural stria moderately deep posteriorly, surface with rows of rather coarse punctures, those of the striæ and intervals equal, color castaneous, suture and margin darker. Metasternum and abdomen obsoletely punctate and alutaceous. Length .10 inch; 2.5 mm.

Male.—Anterior tarsus of male dilated, middle tarsus even broader, posterior femur with outer condyle unciform, the tibia slightly arcuate and a little broadened at tip. (Pl. VII, fig. 4 a).

From its general appearance this species could only be mistaken for *paludicola*, but the regularity of the elytral punctuation and the sexual characters of the male at once distinguish it.

One ♂, Illinois, cabinet of Dr. Leconte.

A. paludicola Crotch.—Oblong-oval, piceous to castaneous, moderately shining. Head sparsely punctate. Thorax a little more than twice as wide as long, narrowed in front, apex emarginate, sides and base arcuate, hind angles distinct but obtuse, surface sparsely punctate. Elytra as wide at base as the thorax, slightly wider at the middle, sides moderately arcuate, base slightly oblique on each side, humeri rounded, surface rather coarsely and irregularly punctate with traces of a striate arrangement at the sides, sutural stria moderately deeply impressed, feeble at base. Metasternum punctate and alutaceous, abdomen alutaceous. Length .10 inch; 2.5 mm.

Male.—Anterior and middle tarsi feebly dilated, posterior tibiæ slightly arcuate.

Female.—Tarsi simple, tibiæ straight.

This species resembles certain of our small Hyduobius more than it does the typical Anisotoma. Among the species of the latter it most closely approaches *conferta* but here the punctures are in distinct striæ.

Collected at El Cajon near San Diego, California, by Mr. Crotch. It also occurs further north in California.

A. strigata Lec.—Oval, very little oblong, pale castaneous, shining. Head sparsely punctate. Thorax more than twice as wide as long, much narrowed in front, apex emarginate, sides feebly arcuate, base truncate, hind angles obtusely rectangular, surface shining very sparsely finely punctate. Elytra as wide at base as the thorax, not wider posteriorly, sides moderately arcuate, humeri not oblique, sutural stria moderately deeply impressed behind the middle, surface with moderately coarse punctures in regular rows, those of the striæ proper and intervals nearly equal and with oblique grooves uniting the punctures, more evident on the disc near the base. Metasternum and abdomen finely alutaceous. Length .08 inch ; 2 mm.

Male.—Anterior tarsi slightly, middle tarsi feebly dilated, posterior tibiæ straight.

Female.—Tarsi slender.

This is the only species known to us with oblique strigæ on the elytra, in fact it is rather a coarse oblique grooving than a true strigosity such as is seen in *Colenis impunctata*. This character will readily distinguish it from any other known at present.

Occurs in the Lake Superior region and in Colorado.

A. obsoleta Mels.—Broadly oval, rufo-testaceous or pale castaneous, moderately shining, convex. Head sparsely punctate. Thorax more than twice as wide as long, narrowed in front, apex emarginate, sides and base arcuate, hind angles rounded, surface sparsely and finely punctate. Elytra as wide at base as the thorax a little wider posteriorly, form broadly oval, nearly as wide as long, base at sides not oblique, surface substriate, striæ with coarse, deep and closely placed punctures forming eight entire rows without the short subhumeral row, intervals flat or slightly convex, sparsely finely punctulate, the alternate intervals with coarser punctures most evident on the third. Metasternum shining, sparsely punctate. Each abdominal segment with a row of coarse deeply impressed punctures along the basal margin. Length .06—.10 inch ; 1.5—2.5 mm.

Male.—Anterior and middle tarsi feebly dilated, middle tibia slightly arcuate, outer condyle of posterior femur prolonged in a triangular tooth, the femur itself gradually broader from the base to apex, posterior tibia straight but stout. (Pl. VII, fig. 4 b).

Female.—Tarsi slender, middle tibia straight, posterior femur somewhat broader externally but without dilated condyle.

This species is one of a small group in which the eight rows of punctures are entire and attain the base of the elytra without diminution, and there is no trace of a short subhumeral row of punctures which is the beginning of a ninth stria and exists in the vast majority of the species.

The mimicry between this insect and *Cyrtusa blandissima* is complete, and is even carried to the sculpture of the body beneath as well as the male sexual characters. The antennal groove in the Cyrtusa and the mesosternal carina in the present will always distinguish them. In the sculpture of the upper surface they are almost precisely identical.

Occurs from the Atlantic to Colorado and in the south to Texas.

A. ecarinata n. sp.—Oblong, moderately elongate, rufo-testaceous, shining. Head sparsely finely punctate. Antennal club piceous. Mandibles not dentate at middle. Thorax more than twice as wide as long, slightly narrowed in front, apex feebly emarginate, base slightly arcuate, sides moderately arcuate, hind angles rounded, surface sparsely punctate. Elytra a little wider than the thorax, oblong-oval, sides feebly arcuate, surface with eight entire rows of punctures, the external slightly less distinct at base but without subhumeral stria, intervals punctulate, the alternate with very distant slightly coarser punctures. Metasternum coarsely punctured at the sides, abdomen less coarsely and indistinctly punctured. Length .08—.10 inch; 2—2.5 mm.

In the two specimens before me the anterior tarsi are wanting, the male has the middle tibiæ slightly arcuate, the posterior femora stouter than in the female and the hind tibiæ are straight. In the female the middle tibia is straight.

The legs are rather stout and the tibiæ not by any means slender, resembling those of *obsoleta*. The middle tibiæ have three quite strong spines on the outer edge.

The absence of mesosternal carina in this species is certainly a very remarkable character and is otherwise unknown to me in the genus. The general appearance of the antennal club is much like that of Cyrtusa except that the small eighth joint is here distinctly visible. The absence of mandibular tooth is also a departure from the *Anisotoma* type. From these departures from the typical structure of the genus the present species might be separated generically, but it seems to me that it is merely an aberrant form of the present genus, indicating decided affinities in the direction of Cyrtusa rather opposite to those shown by *obsoleta*. Were it not that the antennal grooves are wanting I would have considered it an aberrant Cyrtusa.

Two specimens, western Nevada, Morrison.

The following species has not been identified:

"*A. lateritia* Mann., Bull. Mosc. 1852, ii, p. 345.—Breviter ovata, convexa, rufo-ferruginea, oculis clavaque antennarum nigro-fuscis; thorace transverso, crebre punctato, angulis posticis subrectis; elytris profunde striato punctatis, interstitiis confuse seriato-punctatis. Longit. 1¾ lin.; latit. 1 lin.

"In volatu in insula Sitkha a D. *Holmberg* semel capta."

It appears to be a species resembling *conferta* Lec.

COLENIS Erichs.

Head short, broad, slightly prolonged in front of the eyes, clypeus entirely corneous, truncate. Labrum emarginate, with a basal membranous portion. Mandibles feebly prominent, simple. Last joint of maxillary palpi cylindrical, slightly acuminate. Eyes round moderately prominent. Antennæ arising from under a slight frontal margin, eleven-jointed, first joint stout, oval, second as long but more slender, third equal to the second but more slender, 4—6 short, small, seventh a little larger, eighth small, 9—11 forming a loose oblong mass; head beneath without antennal grooves. Prosternum very short in front of the coxæ, the cavities angulate externally and closed behind. Mesosternum moderately separating the coxæ, carinate. Metasternum rather short, the side pieces narrowly visible, posterior coxæ contiguous. Abdomen with six segments. Legs rather short, tibiæ spinulose externally. Tarsi 5—4—4 in both sexes. Form broadly oval, not contractile.

This genus is more closely allied to Anisotoma than to any other. Erichson and the European authorities following him have described the antennæ as having a three-jointed club, and while the same idea is followed in the above diagnosis it seems to me that the club should be called five-jointed, as it certainly does not differ greatly from that seen in many Liodes.

One species occurs in our fauna.

C. impunctata Lec.—Broadly oval, convex, pale brown or testaceous, shining. Head very minutely strigose. Thorax more than twice as wide as long, much narrowed in front, apex feebly emarginate, base and sides arcuate, hind angles rectangular but not acutely so, surface smooth without sculpture. Elytra broadly oval, nearly as wide as long, sides continuing the curve of the sides of the thorax, sutural stria impressed behind the middle, surface finely transversely strigose. Body beneath nearly smooth. Length .06—.08 inch; 1.5—2 mm. (Pl. VI, fig. 23).

The male is known by the anterior tarsi being slightly dilated, the middle tarsi less so, the posterior femora a little stouter.

Occurs from the Middle States to Florida, Illinois and Tennessee.

CYRTUSA Erichs.

Head short, scarcely prolonged in front of the eyes, clypeus short, slightly emarginate at middle. Labrum deeply emarginate, subbilobed. Mandibles moderately prominent, dentate at middle of inner edge. Eyes round, feebly prominent. Antennæ arising from under a slight frontal ridge, rather short, eleven-jointed, the eighth however rarely visible, joints 7—11 forming a rather abrupt, oblong, flattened club, apparently of four joints from the smallness of the eighth, basal joint of antenna short, stout, second as long or even longer but more slender, third equal to second, 4—6 very short, together not longer than the third; head beneath with distinct grooves for the lodgment of the funiculus of the antennæ formed by the elevation of the side of the buccal cavity on the inner side, and a distinct ridge extending along the margin of the eye on the outer side. Maxillary palpi short, terminal joint cylindrical. Prosternum in front of coxæ very short, the coxal cavities transverse, closed behind. Mesosternum moderately separating the coxæ, vertical between them but not carinate. Metasternum moderate in length, the side pieces narrowly visible, posterior coxæ contiguous. Abdomen with six segments. Legs short, moderately stout, tibiæ spinulose externally but not strongly. Tarsi variable in form, joints 5—5—4 in both sexes. Body short, oval, convex, not contractile.

This genus seems very naturally the intermediate between those genera with the tarsi similar in the sexes and those in which they differ, with strong relationship with Anisotoma especially those species allied to *obsoleta*, it seems also equally close to Liodes and Amphicyllis.

Our species are distinguished in the following manner:

Elytra punctured over the entire surface, the striæ of punctures often entirely obliterated..**picipennis** Lec.
Elytra with striæ of punctures, the intervals smooth and shining.
    Tarsi slender...**blandissima** Zimm.
    Tarsi very short and much compressed..**egena** Lec.
These all belong to the fauna of the Atlantic region.

C. picipennis Lec.—Oval, slightly oblong, castaneous to pale brown, shining. Head punctate. Thorax more than twice as wide as long, narrowed in front, apex emarginate, base arcuate, hind angles distinct but obtuse, sides moderately arcuate, surface sparsely finely punctate. Elytra broadly oval, continuing the curve of the thorax, surface irregularly punctate, sometimes with larger punctures forming faint rows near the sides and suture, sutural stria finely impressed behind the middle. Body beneath punctate, abdomen much more finely. Length .06—.08 inch; 1.5—2 mm.

Male.—Tarsi not dilated. Posterior femur gradually broader from the coxa to the knee, the outer condyle forming an acute dentiform process.

Female.—Posterior femur not dilated and without tooth.

In this species the tarsi are slender, the posterior slightly compressed, the tibiæ are normal, the posterior however less spinulose than the middle.

Occurs from Pennsylvania and New York westward through Michigan to Nevada and Vancouver.

C. blandissima Zimm.—Resembles the preceding in form and color. Head and thorax very sparsely and finely punctate. Elytra with eight entire striæ of moderate punctures, not very densely placed, the intervals flat, very rarely with some fine punctures. Body beneath very coarsely punctate, each abdominal segment with a row of coarse, deep, closely placed punctures along its basal margin. Length .06—.08 inch; 1.5—2 mm. (Pl. VII, fig. 8).

Male.—As in *picipennis*. The inner spur of the middle tibiæ is long and strongly arcuate at its base. (Pl. VII, fig. 8 a).

Female.—As in *picipennis.*

The structure of the legs and tarsi is as in *picipennis.*

Occurs in North Carolina and District of Columbia, where the specimens taken by Mr. Ulke are much larger and finer than the type described by Zimmermann.

C. egena Lec.—Resembles *blandissima* in form and color but is usually smaller and more convex. Head and thorax finely punctulate, less distinctly on the thorax. Elytra with eight rows of very fine punctures moderately closely placed but somewhat irregular in their arrangement, intervals flat, smooth, rarely with a few fine punctures. Metasternum minutely punctulate. abdomen more coarsely but vaguely punctate. Length .04—.06 inch; 1—1.5 mm.

Male.—Tarsi not visibly dilated. Posterior femur broad at tip, the outer condyle prolonged in a hook-like process. Spurs of middle tibiæ short. (Pl. VII, fig. 8 b).

Female.—Femur stout without hook-like process.

This species is remarkable in the shortness of its legs, and especially the broader and shorter middle and hind tibiæ which resemble somewhat those of Saprinus. The tarsi are also unusually short and compressed recalling those of *Cremastochilus Schaumii*. It is evidently our representative of the European *latipes*. With this I unite *impubis* Zimm., which seems merely a smaller specimen.

Occurs from Michigan to Georgia.

ISOPLASTUS n. g.

Head short, broad, not prolonged in front of the eyes, clypeus narrowly emarginate at middle. Labrum short, emarginate. Mandibles moderately prominent not dentate within. Eyes round not prominent. Antennæ arising under a distinct frontal ridge, received in distinct grooves on the under side of the head, ten-jointed, first joint short, cylindrical, second equally stout and longer, third more slender, shorter than the second, 4—7 short, together very little longer than the second, 8—10 forming an abrupt, oval, compressed and rather compact club, the first joint of which is longer, the last smaller and rounded at tip. Maxillary palpi short, last joint cylindrical. Thorax in front emarginate. Prosternum in front of coxæ very short, the cavities angulate externally and closed behind. Mesosternum narrowly separating the coxæ, vertical between them and not carinate. Metasternum short, hind coxæ contiguous. Abdomen with six segments. Legs short, fossorial, femora stout, broader at tip, tibiæ broad, the middle strongly and irregularly spinous, the posterior broad and flat, less spinous. Tarsi short, compressed, 5—5—4 in the male, 5—4—4 female. Body almost hemispherical, slightly contractile.

Among the genera with antennal groove and tarsi dissimilar in the sexes this genus is peculiar in its ten-jointed antennæ with triarticulate club. Superficially it resembles *Cyrtusa blandissima* to such a degree that I find it associated with that species in almost every cabinet.

I. fossor n. sp.—Rather broadly oval, very convex, rufo-testaceous, shining. Head sparsely finely punctulate. Thorax twice as wide as long, narrowed in front, apex emarginate, base arcuate, sides moderately arcuate, hind angles obtuse, surface sparsely and minutely punctulate. Elytra continuing the curve of the thorax, humeri slightly oblique, obtusely rounded, surface with eight rows of fine punctures moderately closely placed, those of the disc somewhat irregular, intervals flat, smooth. Metasternum coarsely punctured at the sides, abdomen obsoletely punctate. Length .06—.08 inch; 1.5—2 mm. (Pl. VII, fig. 10).

Male.—Anterior and middle tarsi slightly stouter, posterior femur with the outer condyle prolonged into an obtusely unciform process. Tarsi 5—5—4.

Female.—Tarsi not broader. Posterior femur broad without unciform process. Tarsi 5—4—4.

Four specimens, Detroit, (Hubbard); District of Columbia, (Ulke).

LIODES Latr.

Head feebly convex, not narrowed behind, received in the emarginate thorax nearly as far as the eyes, beneath with well defined antennal grooves, oblique from the eyes inward. Clypeus slightly prolonged beyond the front and corneous, separated from the front by a well marked impressed suture and a depression on each side. Eyes round, moderately prominent. Labrum short usually truncate in front. Mandibles robust, not prominent, simple. Maxillary palpi slender at base, the terminal joint stout, conical. Antennæ arising under a slight frontal margin, nearly attaining the hind angles of the thorax, eleven-jointed, first joint stout, second nearly as stout but shorter, third slender and longer, 4—6 small, gradually broader, the next five forming an elongate loose club, the second joint of which is smaller. Anterior coxæ closed behind, the prosternum in front very narrow. Mesosternum moderately separating the middle coxæ and usually nearly vertical between them, not carinate. Posterior coxæ contiguous. Abdomen with six segments, the terminal usually small. Legs not long, the tibiæ spinulose externally. Tarsi slender, the first joint of the posterior moderately long, the number of joints variable in the sexes, being 5—5—4 in the male and 5—4—4 female.

I am indebted to Dr. Leconte for the use of a short tabular study of the species of the present genus, prepared by Mr. Frederick Blanchard of Lowell, Massachusetts, in which I find the species well and accurately separated, but the increase in the mass of material before me required the preparation of an entirely new table which is presented below. The characters there used seem sufficiently definite and not to need further explanation.

Elytra with regular striæ of punctures...1.
Elytra with more or less confused striæ, becoming in some species nearly double striæ...2.
Elytra without strial arrangement, punctures confused................................3.
1.—Ninth stria of punctures marginal in the greater part of its length, distant from the margin at base only.
Elytra strongly sinuate at the sides, the ninth stria very distant from margin at base, punctures of striæ rather fine.
Intervals of striæ distinctly punctulate.......................**globosa** Lec.
Intervals of striæ smooth or very nearly so...................**polita** Lec.
Elytra not sinuate at the sides, the ninth stria not very distant at base, punctures of striæ rather coarse, intervals smooth.....**discolor** Mels.
Ninth stria distant from the margin in its entire length, elytra not sinuate.
Blanchardi n. sp.

2.—Ninth stria distant from the margin in its entire length.
    Punctures of striæ rather strong, of intervals fine, scarcely perceptible.

basalis Lec.

    Punctures of striæ fine, those of the intervals quite evident.

obsoleta n. sp.

    Ninth stria marginal, distant from the margin for a short distance at base
     only, punctures of discal striæ much confused forming nearly double
    striæ...**geminata** n. sp.

3.—Punctures of elytra much confused without distinct strial arrangement, the
    ˋ punctures rather coarse but unequal................................**confusa** n. sp.

The last is the only species thus far known peculiar to the Pacific
region. A variety of *globosa* occurs with it but but with these exceptions the species are peculiar to the Atlantic region, our total being
slightly in excess of the European list, the genus being thus far confined to our own and that continent.

L. globosa Lec.—Broadly oval, very little longer than wide, convex,
piceous-black, shining. Head and thorax punctulate, the latter much more
sparsely and finely. Hind angles of thorax rectangular, sometimes slightly
obtuse. Elytra oval, not longer than wide at base, the latter on each side
scarcely oblique, the humeri distinct, sides when viewed laterally sinuate
behind the middle, disc with eight entire striæ of moderate punctures, the
ninth short, distant from the margin at base but becoming confused and
joining the margin in front of the middle, intervals sparsely punctulate, the
alternate with scarcely evident coarser punctures, distantly placed. Metasternum coarsely punctate, abdomen more finely and sparsely. Length .12—
.14 inch; 3—3.5 mm.

Male.—Anterior and middle tarsi very slightly dilated. Posterior femora
with a minute denticle at middle.

Female.—Tarsi slender. Posterior femora simple.

Var. **globosa.**—Color entirely piceous-black, sometimes with the legs and
under side paler.

Var. **bicolor.**—Piceous-black, head, thorax and scutellum orange-red, body
beneath and legs rufo-piceous. Occurs in Nevada.

In this species the striæ are not as regular as is usual in this
group although not at all approaching the irregularity of the others.
I do not see any good reason for separating the second variety as a
species, the color being the only difference. I have seen both sexes
of the two forms.

Occurs in the northern part of the Atlantic region extending to
Nevada, and as far south as Kentucky.

L. polita Lec.—Hemispherical, a little longer than wide, piceous-black,
shining. Head very minutely and sparsely punctulate. Thorax smooth, hind
angles rectangular. Elytra not longer than wide at base, humeri distinct,
surface with eight entire striæ of moderate punctures, not closely placed, the
ninth distant from the margin at base but joining it at middle, intervals
smooth, the alternate with distant punctures, sides of elytra when viewed

laterally rather deeply sinuate. Body beneath coarsely but sparsely punctate. Length .12—.14 inch; 3—3.5 mm.

Male.—The tarsi are scarcely at all dilated. The posterior femur has on the lower edge at middle, a slight tubercle similar to that observed in the anterior femora of some *Choleva.*

Female.—Tarsi slender. Femur simple.

This species can only be mistaken for *globosa*, but the less punctate surface will readily distinguish it.

In its distribution this species is more southern than *globosa*, all the specimens seen being from Virginia, Kentucky and Georgia.

L. discolor Mels.—Hemispherical, very little longer than wide, piceous-black above, rufo-piceous beneath, shining. Head and thorax impunctate, the latter with rectangular hind angles. Elytra as wide as long, sides when viewed laterally very feebly sinuate, surface with eight entire striæ of moderately coarse and rather closely placed punctures, the ninth stria distant from the margin at base, confluent with it slightly behind the middle, intervals flat, smooth, the alternate with distant coarse punctures. Body beneath obsoletely sparsely punctate. Length .10—.12 inch; 2.5—3 mm.

Male.—Anterior tarsi moderately dilated, the first joint quite broad, middle tarsi less dilated, posterior femora simple.

Female.—Tarsi very slender.

Occurs from Massachusetts and Canada to Virginia.

L. Blanchardi n. sp.—Hemispherical, piceous-black, very shining. Head very minutely punctulate. Thorax with hind angles rectangular, surface impunctate. Elytra scarcely at all sinuate when viewed laterally, surface with nine entire striæ of moderate punctures, not very closely placed, the ninth stria being entire and equidistant from the margin in its entire length, intervals smooth, shining, the alternate with distant punctures. Body beneath sparsely punctate. Length .08—.10 inch; 2—2.5 mm.

Male.—Anterior tarsi very feebly dilated. Posterior femora with a minute denticle at middle of lower margin.

Female.—Tarsi slender. Femora simple.

In this species the surface is quite as polished as in *Phalacrus.* It could only be mistaken for *discolor*, but the position of the ninth stria would at once distinguish it.

Occurs at Tewksbury, Massachusetts, collected by Mr. F. W. Blanchard who recognized its value as a species.

L. obsoleta n. sp. (Blanchard mss.)—Oval, very convex, somewhat narrower posteriorly, piceous-black, very shining. Head sparsely finely punctulate. Thorax very minutely and distantly punctulate, hind angles rectangular. Elytra with the margin when viewed laterally slightly sinuate, the surface with nine entire striæ of rather fine confused punctures, having a tendency to form double rows, the ninth although confused distant from the margin even at its tip, intervals minutely sparsely punctulate, the alternate with slightly larger punctures distantly placed. Body beneath sparsely punctate. Length .08—.12 inch; 2—3 mm.

Male.—Anterior tarsi slightly dilated. Posterior femora with a small denticle at middle of lower edge.

Female.—Tarsi slender. Femur simple.

Closely resembles *Blanchardi* and differs only in the confused striæ and punctulate intervals.

Occurs from New Hampshire and Canada to Virginia.

L. basalis Lec.—Broadly oval, convex, shining, piceous-black, elytra either entirely orange-red or with a humeral space of variable size of that color. Head and thorax minutely sparsely punctulate. Elytra distinctly sinuate on the sides when viewed laterally, surface with eight entire striæ of rather coarse much confused punctures, the ninth stria distant from the margin at base becoming much confused and joining the margin at middle, intervals scarcely visibly punctulate, the alternate with distant coarser punctures. Body beneath sparsely punctate. Length .10 inch : 2.5 mm.

Male.—Anterior and middle tarsi dilated moderately. The posterior femur flat beneath without tubercle or tooth.

Female.—Tarsi slender.

As already noted this species varies in the color of the elytra, usually there is a narrow basal red space extending from the humeri to near the suture while in others the elytra may become entirely red. These latter are the *dichroa* Lec. It is possible that black varieties of this species may occur which will then closely resemble *discolor* except in the irregularity of the elytral striæ. Excepting in color it also resembles *obsoleta*, but the punctures of the striæ are here coarser and the finer punctures of the intervals barely visible.

Occurs from the Middle States north and as far west as Illinois.

L. geminata n. sp. (Blanchard mss.)—Broadly oval, very convex, slightly narrower behind, piceous-black, shining. Head sparsely minutely punctulate. Thorax smooth, hind angles rectangular. Elytra distinctly sinuate on the sides when viewed laterally, surface with eight rows of very much confused punctures becoming almost double series, the ninth very short, and uniting with the margin very close to the humeri, intervals very minutely punctulate. Body beneath distinctly alutaceous, sparsely punctate. Length .12—.14 inch ; 3—3.5 mm. (Pl. VII, fig. 7).

Male.—Anterior and middle tarsi distinctly dilated. Posterior femur channeled beneath but without tooth or tubercle.

I have seen but two males of this species which approach in size *globosa* and *polita* but have a form more nearly resembling Tritoma (*Cyrtotriplax* Cr.). The characters in the table are sufficient to distinguish it from any at present known.

Occurs from Massachusetts to Virginia and Illinois.

L. confusa n. sp.—Broadly oval, not very convex, piceous-black, humeri reddish, shining. Head very sparsely punctulate. Thorax scarcely perceptibly punctulate. Elytra with the sutural stria moderately deeply impressed, the

300

300 GEO. H. HORN, M. D.

entire surface rather coarsely punctate without traces of strial arrangement, sides of elytra slightly sinuate. Legs rufo-piceous. Body beneath distinctly alutaceous and sparsely punctate. Length .14 inch; 3.5 mm.

Male.—Anterior and middle tarsi dilated. Posterior femora slightly flattened beneath not dentate.

A very distinct species by the absence of any attempt at a strial arrangement of the punctures.

One specimen, western Nevada.

AGATHIDIUM Illig.

Head flat, quadrangular, received in the emarginate thorax as far as the eyes, and with well defined oblique antennal grooves beneath. Clypeus either slightly prolonged, continuous with the front or emarginate and partly membranous. Labrum short, rounded in front. Mandibles simple, the left sometimes prolonged or horned in the male. Maxillary palpi short, clavate, the basal joint very slender, the terminal conical. Eyes oval, not prominent. Antennæ arising under a frontal margin, eleven-jointed, first joint stout, moderate in length, second nearly as stout but shorter, third more slender and longer (except *dentigerum*) than the second, joints 4—8 small, gradually broader, 9—11 forming an oblong, rather loose club. Anterior coxal cavities angulate externally, closed behind. Mesosternum variably separating the coxæ and subcarinate or simple. Metasternum rather short the side pieces narrowly visible, posterior coxæ contiguous. Abdomen with six segments. Legs rather slender but not long, tibiæ not spinulose externally, the spurs small. Tarsi slender and varying between the sexes in the number of joints, being always 5—5—4 in the males and 5—4—4 or 4—4—4 in the females.

The clypeus presents several important modifications. In three species (*sexstriatum, bistriatum* and *estriatum*), that member is entirely corneous and distinctly prolonged beyond the sides of the front. In *concinnum* and *rotundulum* the margin of front and clypeus is continuous without perceptible membranous border, and with membranous border in *exiguum, dentigerum, californicum* and *revolvens*. In *oniscoides, politum, pulchrum* and *difforme*, the clypeus is broadly emarginate and the emargination supplied with a membranous space. The last three it will be observed have the left mandible larger in the male.

These modifications of the structure of the clypeus from that form in which the middle is prominent to that in which the middle is partly membranous, unite in one genus all the important modifications which are observed in the entire family, and indicate that they should not be considered of any value in a generic point of view.

Under *politum* will be found some remarks on the latter character.

The mesosternum has two important modifications which need no further mention than that made in the synoptic table.

A little variation occurs in the antennæ in the length of the third joint as well as in the size of the seventh which is sometimes a little

larger than the eighth, and the antenna then approaches the structure
seen in Liodes.

All the species are more or less contractile, some of them very
feebly so. In the first four species of the table the contractile power
is perfect, so that the specimens roll themselves into a very convex
lenticular mass with the legs retracted and completely concealed. The
greater the contractility the more arcuate the base of the thorax and
the humeri of the elytra more oblique. In all our species the base
of the thorax is foliaceous and overlaps the base of the elytra, but
Lacordaire says that the base of the one is sometimes applied against
the base of the other.

Sexual characters other than those found in the tarsi do not occur
except in *dentigerum*. In the males the tarsi are always 5—5—4,
and in the females 5—4—4 or 4—4—4. The last only occurs in the
group with prominent clypeus.

Fourteen species are now known to us distributed in every part of
our territory, although the species do not have the extended range
observed in those of Anisotoma. A comparison of the number now
known with those described in the European lists suggests the proba-
bility of having but few additions to our lists in the future.

Typical specimens of all the species excepting *oniscoides* and *mandibulatum* have been examined, the first being unnecessary while the
synonymy of the second seems quite evident.

The following table will, I think, enable the known species to be
determined with ease, with the assistance of the descriptions, the
latter having in many cases been abbreviated by comparisons where
repetition seemed unnecessary.

A.—Mesosternum continuous on the same plane with the metasternum, moder-
        ately separating the middle coxæ and subcarinate in front.
Body perfectly contractile, metasternum with an oblique ridge on each side,
     limiting a shallow concavity for the reception of the front and
     middle legs in repose.
    Elytra polished, impunctate.
      Third joint of antennæ longer than the second. Posterior femora of
        male simple.
        Larger species, sutural stria very fine..................**oniscoides** Beauv.
        Smaller species, sutural stria moderately impressed...**exiguum** Mels.
      Third joint of antennæ not longer than the second. Posterior femora of
        male toothed near the tip.
        Small species, sutural stria wanting..................**dentigerum** n. sp.
    Elytra punctulate, otherwise as in *exiguum*............**californicum** n. sp.
Body very imperfectly contractile, metasternum without raised oblique line.
     Elytra substriate and punctate..................**revolvens** Lec.

B.—Mesosternum vertical between the coxæ which it narrowly separates, not carinate in front.

Hind angles of thorax distinct almost rectangular, humeri very little oblique, body feebly contractile. Clypeus slightly more prominent than the sides of the front.

Elytra with moderately coarse punctures and six, more or less regular, striæ on the disc. Thorax sparsely punctulate...**sexstriatum** n. sp.

Elytra with coarse punctures and but two feeble striæ. Thorax smooth, impunctate..**bistriatum** n. sp.

Elytra very irregularly punctate with coarse and fine punctures intermixed. Thorax sparsely punctulate............**estriatum** n. sp.

Hind angles of thorax broadly rounded, body contractile.

Clypeus prominent at middle. Elytra punctulate...**repentinum** n. sp.

Clypeus truncate at middle, entirely corneous.

Elytra coarsely punctate................................**concinnum** Mann.

Surface absolutely smooth. Elytra without sutural stria.

rotundulum Mann.

Clypeus emarginate and partly membranous. Left mandible of male prolonged.

Body feebly convex, finely and equally punctulate.

angulare Mann.

Body very convex and contractile.

Surface very smooth, rarely with feeble trace of punctuation.

politum Lec.

Elytra distinctly punctulate, elytra with yellow oblique spots, sometimes however entirely piceous.... ....**pulchrum** Lec.

Surface more evidently punctate, thorax punctulate.

difforme Lec.

A. oniscoides Beauv.—Body perfectly contractile, black or piceous, entirely impunctate, smooth and shining. Thorax nearly twice as wide as long, base and posterior portion of the sides continuously arcuate, apex deeply emarginate the anterior angles broadly rounded. Elytra when viewed from above almost truly circular in outline, the margin when viewed from the side continuously arcuate without angulation, sutural stria very finely impressed. Metasternum finely alutaceous, sparsely obsoletely punctulate, and with an oblique elevated line on each side, the two meeting at middle, abdomen more rugulose, sparsely pubescent. Mesosternum continuous with the metasternum and obtusely carinate in front. Length extended .14—.16 inch; 3.5—4 mm. (Pl. VII, figs. 11, 12, 13).

Male.—Anterior tarsi slightly dilated. Tarsi 5—5—4.

Female.—Anterior tarsi slender. Tarsi 5—4—4.

This species is so perfectly contractile that the legs are completely hidden when in that state. The elevated line on the metasternum is the posterior limit of a slight concavity which accommodates the anterior and middle legs in contraction.

A. globatile Lec. is merely a smaller form.

Occurs over the territory east of the Mississippi from Canada to Georgia.

A. exiguum Mels.—Resembles a diminutive form of the preceding species and is known only by its small size, sutural stria more deeply impressed, lateral margin of elytra slightly angulate, body less perfectly contractile. Length extended .08—.10 inch; 2—2.5 mm.

Varieties occur in this species in which some have the elytra absolutely smooth, others punctulate, they are not however distinct.

Sexual characters as in *oniscoides*.

Occurs with the preceding, and in Colorado.

A. dentigerum n. sp.—Smaller than *exiguum* and perfectly contractile as in *oniscoides*. Antennæ with third joint evidently shorter than the second. Surface smooth, shining and impunctate, sutural stria entirely wanting. Body beneath as in *oniscoides*. Length .06—.07 inch; 1.5—1.75 mm.

Male.—Anterior tarsi slightly dilated. Posterior femur rather slender with a triangular tooth near the outer condyle. Tarsi 5—5—4.

Female.—Tarsi slender, femora simple. Tarsi 5—4—4.

Two specimens, Stone Creek, Lee Co., Virginia, (Schwarz).

A. californicum n. sp.—Closely resembling *exiguum*, similarly contractile. Head and thorax microscopically alutaceous, elytra sparsely but very distinctly punctulate, sutural stria moderately deeply impressed and extending from the apex beyond the middle. Length .08—.10 inch; 2—2.5 mm.

Sexual characters as in *exiguum*.

When viewed laterally the margin of the elytra is more distinctly angulate than in *exiguum* but not more so than in *dentigerum*.

Occurs in California, Nevada and Washington Territory.

A. revolvens Lec.—Broadly oval, piceous, shining, semi-contractile. Head sparsely finely punctulate. Thorax less than twice as wide as long, narrowed in front, apex deeply emarginate, base broadly arcuate, sides not continuously arcuate with the base, hind angles distinct but rounded, surface sparsely very finely punctulate. Elytra oval longer than wide, base at sides oblique, humeri rounded, sutural stria rather deeply impressed from middle to apex, surface substriate, sparsely punctulate, the punctures coarser and denser than on the thorax. Mesosternum oblique, finely carinate in front. Metasternum without oblique line, surface alutaceous sparsely punctate. Abdomen sparsely punctate. Length extended .14 inch; 3.5 mm.

Sexual characters as in *oniscoides*.

This species from the structure of the base of the thorax is far less contractile than the preceding species. In some specimens, particularly the males, there is a tendency in the seventh joint of the antennæ to become larger than the eighth, showing an approach toward Liodes which is also indicated by the less contractile power.

Occurs from Canada to Vancouver.

A. sexstriatum n. sp.—Oblong-oval, moderately convex, scarcely at all contractile, piceous, thorax orange-red, shining. Head sparsely finely punctulate. Thorax more than twice as wide as long, much narrowed in front, sides arcuate, apex deeply emarginate, base feebly arcuate, hind angles subrectangular, not prominent, surface obsoletely sparsely punctulate. Elytra oval slightly longer than wide, not wider than the thorax, sides gradually arcuately narrowing to apex, surface with six moderately well-defined striæ of coarse punctures, the intervals and sides of elytra with finer punctures not densely placed. Body beneath sparsely punctulate, shining. Length .08 inch; 2 mm.

Male.—Anterior and middle tarsi moderately dilated. Tarsi 5—5—4.

Female.—Tarsi slender 4—4—4.

Occurs in western Nevada, (Morrison). An easily known species.

A. bistriatum n. sp.—Broadly oval, convex, semi-contractile, piceous, moderately shining. Head sparsely punctulate, clypeus rufous. Thorax more than twice as wide as long, narrowed in front, base broadly arcuate, sides moderately arcuate, hind angles rectangular but not prominent, surface impunctate. Elytra broadly oval, nearly as wide as long, base at sides slightly oblique, humeri very distinct, sutural stria moderately impressed, surface moderately coarsely but not densely punctate with two feeble striæ of punctures on the disc. Body beneath sparsely punctulate. Length .10—.12 inch; 2.5—3 mm.

Male.—Anterior and middle tarsi moderately dilated. Tarsi 5—5—4.

Female.—Tarsi slender 4—4—4.

This species resembles some of the forms of *concinnum* but the latter is more contractile, hind angles rounded, elytra without striæ and the female tarsi differently formed.

Occurs in western Nevada, (Morrison).

A. estriatum n. sp.—Broadly oval, convex, semi-contractile, piceous, shining, thorax orange-red. Thorax more than twice as wide as long, narrowed in front, apex feebly emarginate, base and sides arcuate, hind angles obtusely rectangular, surface very sparsely and minutely punctulate. Elytra oval, a little longer than wide, base at sides slightly oblique, humeri distinct, sutural stria moderately impressed posteriorly, surface moderately densely but irregularly punctured with coarse and finer punctures intermixed. Body beneath sparsely finely punctulate. Length .10 inch; 2.5 mm.

Male.—Anterior and middle tarsi slightly dilated. Tarsi 5—5—4.

Female.—Unknown.

This species has some resemblance to *concinnum* and *angulare*, but is intermediate in punctuation and differs from both in the hind angles of the thorax.

One specimen, Garland, Colorado, (Schwarz).

A. repentinum n. sp.—Oval, convex, contractile, piceous, shining. Head sparsely punctulate, clypeus slightly prolonged at middle, truncate at tip and corneous. Thorax more than twice as wide as long, hind angles broadly rounded, surface sparsely punctulate. Elytra oval, very little longer than wide, humeri oblique forming a distinct angle with the sides, sutural stria extremely fine but attaining the middle, surface very distinctly punctate. Body beneath sparsely punctate. Length .08 inch; 2 mm.

I have seen but one ♀ of this species. It might readily be confounded with *difforme* but differs by the form of the clypeus and the more finely impressed sutural stria. For the discovery of this species I am indebted to Mr. F. Blanchard of Lowell, Massachusetts.

Occurs in the White Mountains, New Hampshire.

A. concinnum Mann.—Broadly oval, very convex, contractile, color variable from testaceous to piceous. Head sparsely finely punctulate. Thorax more than twice as wide as long, narrowed in front, apex moderately emarginate, sides moderately, base strongly arcuate, hind angles broadly rounded, surface sparsely obsoletely punctulate. Elytra very broadly oval, scarcely longer than wide, base on each side slightly oblique, humeri rounded, surface coarsely not densely punctured, sutural stria long, moderately deeply impressed. Body beneath sparsely punctulate, abdomen a little more coarsely. Length .08—.12 inch ; 2—3 mm.

Male.—Anterior and middle tarsi slightly dilated. Tarsi 5—5—4.

Female.—Tarsi slender 5—4—4.

With this species I unite *effluens* Mann., after a comparison of types from that author. The punctuation varies somewhat but not beyond the ordinary limits.

Occurs from California and Nevada northward to Alaska.

A. rotundulum Mann.—Oval, very convex, contractile, piceous, margins often paler. Surface absolutely smooth, elytra without sutural stria. Thorax as in *concinnum*. Base of elytra very oblique and forming a very distinct angle with the sides. Body beneath sparsely punctulate. Length fully extended .08 inch; 2 mm.

Sexual characters unknown, the two specimens from Mannerheim now before me are in such condition that I cannot safely determine the number of tarsal joints.

Two specimens, Alaska.

A. angulare Mann.—Broadly oval, not very convex, semi-contractile, piceous, moderately shining. Head minutely punctulate. Thorax much more than twice as wide as long, narrower in front, apex feebly emarginate, sides and base arcuate, hind angles rounded, surface moderately densely but very minutely punctulate. Elytra oval, a little longer than wide, base on each side slightly oblique, humeri distinct, sutural stria long, moderately impressed, surface finely but not densely punctulate. Body beneath very sparsely finely punctulate. Length .14 inch; 3.5 mm.

Male.—Anterior and middle tarsi slightly dilated. Tarsi 5—5—4.

Female.—Tarsi slender 5—4—4.

As in all the species which follow the margin of the front is apparently emarginate, the front edge of the clypeus being membranous. The mandibles of male are normal.

Two specimens, Alaska and Colorado.

A. politum Lec.—Oval, very convex, contractile, color variable from rufo-ferruginous to piceous, shining. Head smooth. Thorax more than twice as wide as long, narrowed in front, apex moderately deeply emarginate, sides

and base arcuate, hind angles broadly rounded, surface smooth. Elytra oval,
nearly as wide as long, base on each side oblique, humeral angles distinct
but obtuse, sutural stria moderately long, finely impressed, surface smooth,
in the pale specimens sparsely punctulate when examined under a high
power. Body beneath sparsely punctulate. Length .08—.10 inch; 2—2.5 mm.
(Pl. VII, fig. 14).

Male.—Anterior and middle tarsi slightly dilated. Tarsi 5—5—4. Left mandible either much prolonged or with a horn-like process from the upper side.

Female.—Tarsi slender 5—4—4. Mandibles similar not prolonged.

After an examination of a large number of specimens I find that
the elytra are absolutely smooth in some and microscopically punctulate in others, the specimens which are totally black being the
smoother. The males also vary in the structure of the left mandible,
there being every gradation between the prolonged mandible and that
in which the prolongation becomes a distinct horn arising from its
upper edge. This variation can readily be shown in *pulchrum* which
seems to be abundant, and in this I have a male not differing appreci-
ably in its mandibles from the female. As this mandibular character
is a normal structure which closely approaches the borders of mon-
strosity, its variation cannot be assumed to have specific value.

A. parvulum Lec., seems to be merely a small form of the same.

Occurs from Pennsylvania to Missouri, and from Canada to Kentucky.

A. pulchrum Lec.—Resembles *politum* in form, elytra always distinctly
sparsely punctulate. Head piceous, often with a paler vertical spot. Thorax
reddish-yellow with large round, discal, piceous space. Elytra piceous, each
with two large, oblique, yellowish spots of variable size and shape. Length
.10—.12 inch; 2.5—3 mm.

Sexual characters as in *politum.*

The color varies greatly so that the head and thorax may be
entirely piceous and the elytral spots comparatively small, or the
spots may extend and become confluent. *A. mandibulatum* Mann.,
is without much doubt the same species.

Occurs in California and also in the White Mountains, New Hampshire, (Austin), but I have not seen any from intermediate points
except Kentucky, (Dury).

A. difforme Lec.—Similar in form to *politum* but a little more elongate,
piceous, moderately shining, margin of thorax and a vague oblique stripe on
each elytron. Head very obviously punctulate. Thorax sparsely and finely
punctulate. Elytra with sutural stria moderately deeply impressed and extending two thirds to base, surface sparsely but very evidently punctate. Body
beneath sparsely punctulate. Length .08 inch; 2 mm.

Male.—First two joints only of anterior tarsus slightly dilated. Tarsi 5—5—4.
Female.—Tarsi slender 5—4—4.

This species is so much more obviously punctate that there need be no difficulty in separating it from the preceding two species. In nearly all the specimens I have seen the sides of the thorax are rufopiceous, and a vague paler space on each elytron extending from the humeri to the suture at apex.

Occurs in the White Mountains, (Austin), and the Lake Superior region.

Here seems a fit place to reproduce Say's description of an unknown ' species. It is certainly not an Agathidium, and may be either an Anisotoma or Hydnobius. I have placed it doubtfully under *II. Matthewsii*.

" *Agathidium pallidum.*—Body yellowish-testaceous; elytra with very minute transverse lines.

" Inhabits Missouri.

" Body oval, convex, yellowish-testaceous, glabrous; head with a few hairs beneath the edge; eyes prominent, hemispherical, black; palpi subulate; antennæ hirsute, clavate; club oblong, perfoliate; second joint of club minute; thorax impunctured; scutel minute; elytra rugose in transverse very minute lines; thighs with very minute spines above; tibia with prominent rigid spines.

" Length more than three-twentieths of an inch.

" A simple specimen occurred under wood, at Engineer Cantonment."

Although the Anisotomini with similarly sculptured elytra are few I am entirely unable to make this fit any known to me, the nearest approach being as above stated.

AGLYPTUS Lec.

Head broad and flat, with distinct antennal grooves beneath, clypeus not prolonged, finely margined in front, the suture not visible. Labrum short, broad, emarginate. Mandibles not prominent, simple. Eyes oval, rather coarsely granulated beneath. Antennæ arising under a slight frontal margin, eleven-jointed, first joint stout, second nearly as stout but longer, third more slender than the second and shorter, 4—5—6 short but longer than wide and together a little longer than the third, seventh broader, eighth smaller than the seventh, last three joints forming an oblong club, the terminal broader and longer than the preceding. Maxillary palpi slender, first joint short, second and third nearly equal and not stouter than the first, terminal joint slender, acute at tip, nearly equal in length to the preceding two. Prosternum very short in front of the coxæ, the cavities angulate externally and closed behind. Mesosternum moderately separating the coxæ, vertical between them and rather strongly carinate. Metasternum moderate in length, the coxæ contiguous. Abdomen with six segments, the terminal scarcely visible. Legs rather short, the femora stout, tibiæ slender, not spinulose externally and with very minute tibial spurs. Body oval, convex, partially contractile. Tarsi slender the anterior dilated in the male, these four-jointed, the middle and posterior three-jointed. Tarsi of female three jointed on all, the first and last joints moderately long and equal, the second short.

With the antennal grooves beneath the head and the dissimilarity of the tarsi in the sexes, there can be no doubt that this genus should be placed near Agathidium and not Colenis. The antennal club is however somewhat like that of the latter genus, so that there may be some doubt as to whether it should be called three- or five-jointed, it is in much the same condition that we find in several species of Agathidium in which the seventh joint is a little larger than the eighth.

The number of the tarsal joints in the male is a repetition in the present series of genera of the same character in Agaricophagus, in which however the tarsi are similar in the two sexes. That they are three-jointed on all the tarsi in the female has been verified by an examination under the compound microscope, a matter rather difficult to do in so small an insect.

A. lævis Lec.—Oval, very convex, very little longer than wide, piceous, shining, surface without sculpture. Thorax with margin and base translucent, hind angles rectangular. Body beneath rufous, smooth. Length extended .04— .06 inch; 1—1.5 mm. (Pl. VII, fig. 15).

Male.—Anterior tarsi moderately dilated, four-jointed, middle and posterior tarsi three-jointed.

Female.—Tarsi slender, three-jointed on all the feet.

The form of this insect is that of a diminutive Agathidium resembling *rotundulum* or *politum*.

Occurs in Canada, Illinois, Georgia, Louisiana, but rare.

Tribe VI.—*Clambini*.

Anterior coxæ conical, moderately prominent, contiguous, with moderate trochantin, the cavities angulate externally and closed behind. Middle coxæ separated by the mesosternum in *Empelus* and by the fine carina in the other genera. Posterior coxæ contiguous with plates covering the thighs, partially in *Empelus* or completely in *Clambus* and *Calyptomerus*. Antennæ of eleven, ten or nine joints variably inserted, either contiguously to the eyes (in *Clambus*) or distant, but not under a frontal margin. Tarsi four-jointed, tibiæ without spurs.

The structure of the posterior coxæ affords the only means of separating this tribe from the rest of the family as a whole. By the structure of the anterior coxæ and their cavities the Anisotomini are the only close allies.

The posterior coxæ in two of the genera have quite broad plates arcuately narrowed within which cover completely the posterior legs in repose. In Empelus however the plate is very narrow on the outer part of the coxa and dilated only at the articulation somewhat after the manner of certain Elateridæ. In two of the genera the elytra are not margined and there is no separation of any epipleural portion. Empelus however reverts to the general type with distinct margin and epipleuræ.

In Clambus and Calyptomerus the middle coxæ are very narrowly separated by a thin lamina while in Empelus the separation is well marked. In the first two the mesosternum is almost hidden and the metasternum is concave in front, the depression limited behind by a well marked arcuate edge. In Empelus however there is no such structure, the mesosternum is quite distinct and the metasternum not concave. This excavation of the metasternum has already been foreshadowed in certain Agathidium (*oniscoides*, etc.), and has already been described and its meaning indicated.

One of the most curious characters in the tribe is found in the method of insertion of the antennæ. In Empelus the sides of the front, a little distance in advance of the eyes, are simply sinuate, the basal joint is here inserted and the antennæ in repose pass under the head to a distinct groove. In Clambus there is apparently a triangular notch, but on closer examination it will be observed that the sides of the head are acutely margined and that portion of the acute margin appears to pass under the head and become continuous with the ridge which defines the inner edge of the antennal groove. The antennæ arise close to the eyes in Clambus. In Calyptomerus however the structure is quite distinct. The antennæ arise at a distance in front of the eye midway between it and the middle of the front, the sides of the head are acute as in Clambus, an edge or margin passing forward from the front of the eye while the frontal margin passes backward and dips under the other, continuing in a ridge beneath the head as in Clambus. Between the two ridges thus formed the antennæ arise and the first joint is concealed and may readily escape detection.

The manner in which the antennæ are disposed of beneath the head requires special mention. Attention has already been directed to the ridge which is the inner limit of the antennal grooves or cavities beneath the head. In Empelus and Clambus this ridge is nearly straight and not very distant from the inner edge of the eye. In the former genus the stem of the antenna lies close against this ridge when in repose, the clavicular portion being then bent and resting in an arcuate groove which crosses the gula from one side to the other, the tips of the two clubs probably touching, (Pl. VII, fig. 19 c). A similar condition exists in Clambus except that there is a median gular ridge and on each side a shallow fossa in which the club rests, (Pl. VII, fig. 19 a). In Calyptomerus however the case is different. The head being much larger and broader and the antennæ arising so much in front of the eye, the ridge in passing beneath the head is arcuate inward leaving between it and the eye a wide space, the antenna is consequently received on the side of the head beneath and within the eye, and is curved in a somewhat spiral manner and does not reach the gula at all, (Pl. VII, fig. 19 b).

Finally the abdomen varies in the number of the segments as will be seen in the table.

The genera may be thus separated :

Elytra margined at the sides with distinct epipleuræ. Coxal plates narrow.
  Antennæ 11-jointed, club 3-jointed. Moderately distant from the eyes at base.
    Abdomen with seven segments...**Empelus.**
Elytra not margined at the sides, without epipleuræ. Coxal plates wide.
  Antennæ 10-jointed, club 2-jointed. Arising at a distance from the eyes.
    Abdomen with six segments...**Calyptomerus.**
  Antennæ 9-jointed, club 2-jointed. Arising close to the eyes.
    Abdomen with five segments visible...**Clambus.**

Empelus and *Calyptomerus* have the elytra slightly prolonged and obliquely truncate, in *Clambus* rounded at tip not prolonged.

In addition to the above genera M. Mulsant has described *Loricaster* (Opusc. Ent. xii, 1861, p. 139), said to have wide coxal plates, three-jointed antennal club with non-contractile body. Through the kindness of M. Henri Jekel I have been enaabled to examine a specimen, and find it in every respect a Clambus resembling our *C. puberulus.*

EMPELUS Lec.

Head moderate in size, not rapidly narrowing behind, front moderately long, oval, clypeus not distinct. Labrum small almost concealed. Mandibles as in *Clambus.* Maxillary palpi moderately long, first joint very small, second long and slender, third small and oval, fourth as long as second, oval, obtuse at tip, rather flat with the under side concave. Eyes longitudinally oval, moderately granulated. Antennæ arising at a distance from the eyes, in a slight sinuation of the sides of the front, the stem received in very distinct antennal grooves beneath the eyes, the club received beneath the gula in an arcuate depression which extends from one side to the other; eleven-jointed, first joint oval, flat, suddenly narrowed at base, second less stout, much shorter and oval, 3—6 slender and long, gradually shorter, 7—8 small, rounded, 9—11 forming an oblong club, the last joint longer, oval at tip. Thorax beneath as in *Clambus.* Scutellum small. Mesosternum moderately separating the coxæ and very finely carinate. Metasternum moderately long not excavated in front. Posterior coxæ contiguous, the plate much narrower than in Clambus and dilated over the femoral articulation only. Abdomen with seven distinct segments (at least in the male). Elytra distinctly margined at the sides, epipleuræ distinct. Legs slender not long, tibiæ not spinulose and without terminal spurs. Tarsi slender, four-jointed, first three joints subequal, very gradually decreasing in length, last joint very nearly as long as these together. Body winged, feebly contractile.

This genus seems fully to unite, through Aglyptus, the Anisotomini with the present tribe. By its feeble contractile power and entire metasternum it differs strikingly from Clambus and Calyptomerus, and the structure of its maxillary palpi, antennæ, mesosternum and posterior coxæ define it as one of the most distinct genera in the entire family.

One species occurs in our fauna.

E. brunnipennis Mann.—Oblong-oval, moderately convex, feebly contractile, sparsely clothed with extremely fine pubescence, piceous, head and thorax rufous. Head sparsely minutely punctulate. Thorax about twice as wide as long, narrowed in front, apex broadly emarginate, sides feebly arcuate, base broadly arcuate, hind angles distinct but obtuse, surface very minutely punctulate. Elytra oval, gradually narrowed posteriorly, base on each side slightly oblique, humeri obtuse, sides feebly arcuate, apex slightly obliquely truncate, surface very minutely sparsely punctulate. Body beneath and legs rufo-piceous, surface very sparsely punctulate. Length extended .08 inch; 2 mm. (Pl. VII, fig. 16).

The male has the anterior tarsi distinctly broader than the female.

This insect has much more general resemblance to a non-contractile Agathidium than to Clambus.

Occurs in Alaska.

CLAMBUS Fischer.

Head large, broad, rather flat, angulate at the sides and acutely margined, gradually narrowed behind, front oval, at sides before the eyes notched allowing the antennæ to pass beneath the head to an oblique antennal groove which is limited within by a raised line. Clypeus not distinct. Eyes rather large but flattened above and angulate, beneath rather coarsely granulated. Antennæ ciliate, nine-jointed, inserted free at the anterior margin of the eyes, first joint short, stout, oval, second slender and long, third and fourth slender, shorter than the second, 5—7 short, gradually a little broader, 8—9 forming an oval club, the terminal larger. Labrum short, scarcely visible beyond the clypeus. Mandibles short, bifid at tip. Maxillary palpi with first joint very small, second and third stouter, subequal, terminal slender and acute at tip, as long as the two preceding united. Anterior coxæ conical, transverse, contiguous with distinct trochantin, the cavities angulate externally and closed behind, prosternum in front very narrow. Mesosternum very short, carinate between the coxæ which are very transverse. Metasternum moderately long, suddenly concave in front, the concavity limited by an arcuate edge. Posterior coxæ laminate covering the hind thighs completely in repose, the plates arcuately narrowed within. Abdomen with five visible segments only. Legs slender not long, the tibiæ not spinulose and without terminal spurs. Tarsi slender and moderately long, four-jointed, first joint long; equal to the next two which are gradually shorter, the fourth nearly as long as the first. Body globose oval, very convex, perfectly contractile, winged, the under wings well developed, long and ciliate.

In addition to the above characters it will be noticed that the gula is obtusely carinate at middle, and with a shallow fovea on each side for the lodgment of the club of the antennæ, the elytra are not margined at the sides and the epipleuræ are not distinct.

The foregoing description is unusually long from the fact that all preceding authors fail to mention characters which seem of great importance, in view of the system of classification adopted in the preceding pages. The entire structure of Clambus indicates the propriety of retaining it in the present family, although it possesses certain characters at variance with the general structure, while some of the structures here are already foreshadowed in Agathidium and Aglyptus. These genera with Empelus in the present tribe connect Clambus with the general mass of the family.

Erichson held the opinion that these insects should be placed among the Coccinellidæ, while other authors have seen resemblances to the Trichopterygidæ. The first idea seems to have no substantial foundation while the latter has more in its favor,* yet the resemblances are too few and the points of divergence so many that it may be equally dismissed.

Our species are three in number, as follows:

Surface smooth, shining, glabrous, without punctuation or pubescence.

gibbulus Lec.

Surface sparsely pubescent.
Elytra posteriorly moderately densely finely punctulate...**pubernlus** Lec.
Elytra with obsolete, very sparse punctuation.
Humeral angles of elytra rounded..............................**semiunlum** n. sp.
Humeral angles distinct.......................................**vulneratus** Lec.

C. gibbulus Lec.—Globose-oval, piceous-black, shining, surface smooth without punctuation or pubescence. Thorax more than twice as wide as long, sides short strongly arcuate, apex sinuate each side, base strongly arcuate, hind angles rounded, lateral margin more or less diaphanous. Elytra very little longer than wide, humeri rounded. Body beneath smooth with extremely sparse pubescence. Legs and antennæ testaceous. Length extended .04 inch; 1 mm. (Pl. VII, fig. 18).

I have not observed any special sexual differences except that certain specimens seem to have the anterior tarsi broader and are probably males.

Occurs from Canada to Texas.

---

* The under wings are ciliate with long hairs in a manner very similar to that family.

C. puberulus Lec.—Globose-oval, piceous to piceo-testaceous, elytra paler toward the tip. Head and thorax very sparsely minutely punctulate and finely pubescent. Elytra more distinctly punctulate, very sparsely on the disc, gradually more dense to the tip, surface sparsely pubescent. Body beneath sparsely minutely punctulate and pubescent. Legs and antennæ testaceous. Length .04 inch; 1 mm.

Usually a little smaller than the preceding and differing in its punctuation and pubescence.

Occurs from Massachusetts to District of Columbia.

C. vulneratus Lec.—Globose-oval, piceous-black, each elytron with an indistinctly limited rufous space at middle. Head and thorax extremely finely and very sparsely punctulate and pubescent. Elytra with the humeral angles rectangular, surface smooth on the disc, very sparsely punctulate at the sides and near the apex and sparsely pubescent. Body beneath very minutely punctulate and sparsely pubescent. Legs and antennæ testaceous. Length .04 inch; 1 mm.

Easily known by the above characters. The elytral spot is probably not constant, and it is possible that other specimens will show that the elytra may become gradually paler to tip as in *puberulus*.

One specimen, Garland, Colorado.

C. seminulum n. sp.—Closely resembling *puberulus* in form and color and differs only in having the punctuation as in *vulneratus*. The humeral angles of the elytra are rounded as in *puberulus*. Length .04 inch; 1 mm.

Two specimens, Camp Grant, Arizona.

CALYPTOMERUS Redt.

Characters of *Clambus* with the following exceptions: Maxillary palpi with the first joint small, second much stouter, obconical, third much smaller, fourth more slender and nearly equal to the two preceding, obtuse at tip. Antennæ ten-jointed, first joint short and stout, second somewhat globose, as stout as the first, third slender, 4—6 slender, gradually decreasing in length, 7—8 small, nodose, 9—10 forming an oval mass the terminal a little smaller; antennæ arising at a distance in front of the eye in a notch in the side of the front, the antennæ in repose received in broad shallow cavities on the under side of the head between the eyes and the gula. Abdomen with six distinct segments. Elytra slightly prolonged, subtruncate at tip. Body winged. Metasternum very little excavated in front. The eyes are coarsely granulated above and beneath and the tarsi are longer than those of Clambus.

The differences between this genus and the preceding are many and important, and it seems rather remarkable that the insertion of the antennæ at a point so distant from the eyes should have escaped notice in print, as that accurate artist Mr. Jules Migneaux has not failed to represent it in his figure, (Duval, vol. i, pl. 18, fig. 189).

C. oblongulus Mann.—Oblong-oval, convex, contractile, piceo-testaceous, moderately shining, sparsely pubescent. Head large, rapidly narrowing behind the eyes, occiput vaguely transversely impressed, surface sparsely minutely punctulate. Thorax smaller than the head but a little wider, more than twice as wide as long, apex on each side slightly sinuate, sides very short broadly arcuate, base less arcuate, surface sparsely minutely punctulate. Elytra oblong-oval, arcuately narrowing to apex which is obliquely truncate, base slightly oblique on each side, humeri obtuse, surface sparsely minutely punctulate, the punctures denser near the tip, pubescence longer and more evident than on the head and thorax. Body beneath sparsely punctulate, finely pubescent. Length extended .08 inch; 2 mm. (Pl. VII, fig. 17).

The male has the anterior tarsi distinctly broader than in the female.

Occurs in Alaska and at Veta Pass, Colorado.

Bibliography and Synonymy.

NECROPHORUS Fab.

N. carolinus Linn., Mantissa vi, 1771, p. 530.

mediatus Fab., Syst. El. i, p. 334; Leach, Zool. Misc. ii, p. 86, pl. 90, fig. 2 ; Lec. Proc. Acad. 1853, p. 275.

N. americanus Oliv., Ent. ii, 10, p. 6, pl. 1, fig. 3; Lec. loc. cit. p. 276.

grandis Fab., Ent. Syst. i, p. 247; Syst. El. i, p. 334; Herbst, Käfer v, p. 152, pl. 50, fig. 1.

virginicus Fröhl., Naturf. xxvi, p. 123.

N. Sayi Lap., Hist. Nat. ii, p. 2.

lunatus ‖ Lec., loc. cit. p. 277.

luniger Harold, Heft. iv.

N. orbicollis Say, Journ. Acad. v, p. 177; Lec. loc. cit. p. 277.

Halli Kby., Fauna Bor. Am. iv, p. 98.

quadrisignatus Lap., Hist. Nat. ii, p. 1.

N. marginatus Fab., Syst. El. i, p. 334; Lec. loc. cit. p. 275.

N. obscurus Kby., Fauna Bor. Am. iv, p. 97.

Melsheimeri ‡ Lec., loc. cit. p. 275.

N. guttula Motsch., Bull. Mosc. 1845, i, p. 53; Lec. loc. cit. p. 276.

Hecate Bland, Proc. Ent. Soc. Phil. 1865, p. 382.

N. pustulatus Herschel, Illig. Mag. vi, p. 271; Lec. loc. cit. p. 276.

bicolon Newm., Ent. Mag. v, p. 385.

tardus Mann., Bull. Mosc. 1853, iii, p. 170.

var. *Melsheimeri* Kby., Fauna Bor. Am. iv, p. 97.

maritimus Mann., Bull. Mosc. 1843, ii, p. 251.

infodiens Mann., Bull. Mosc. 1853, iii, p. 170.

pollinctor ‖ Mann., loc. cit. p. 169.

confossor Lec., Proc. Acad. 1854, p. 20.

labiatus Motsch., Schrenk Reis. 1860, p. 126.

var. *nigrita* Mann., Bull. Mosc. 1843, ii, p. 251; Lec. Proc. Acad. 1853, p. 276.

N. vespilloides Herbst, Füssl. Archiv. 1784, v, p. 32.

mortuorum Fab., Ent. Syst. i, p. 248.

pygmæus Kby., Faun. Bor. Am. iv, p. 98, pl. 2, fig. 3.

Hebes Kby., loc. cit. p. 96.

defodiens Mann., Bull. Mosc. 1846, ii, p. 513.

var. *pollinctor* Lec., Proc. Acad. 1854, p. 19.

conversator Walker, Nat. in Vanc. ii, 1866, p. 320.

N. tomentosus Weber, Obs. Ent. i, p. 47.

velutinus Fab., Syst. El. i, p. 334; Lec. Proc. Acad. 1853, p. 277.

SILPHA Linn.

S. surinamensis Fab., Syst. Ent. p. 72; Oliv. Ent. ii, II, pl. I, fig. 3; Lec. Proc. Acad. 1853, p. 278.

S. truncata Say, Journ. Acad. iii, p. 193; Lec. Col. Kans. p. 6, pl. 1, fig. 3.

S. lapponica Hbst., Käfer v, p. 209, pl. 52, fig. 4; Kirby, Faun. Bor. Am. iv, p. 100 ; Lec. Proc. Acad. 1853, p. 278.

caudata Say, Journ. Acad. iii, p. 192.

tuberculata Germ., Ins. Spec. Nov. p. 81.

californica Mann., Bull. Mosc. 1843, ii, p. 253.

S. trituberculata Kby., Faun. Bor. Am. iv, p. 101.

sagax Mann., Bull. Mosc. 1853, iii, p. 173.

S. inæqualis Fab., Spec. Ins. i, p. 87; Hbst. Käfer v, p. 185, pl. 41, fig. 2; Oliv. Ent. ii, 11, p. 14, pl. 2, fig. 20; Lec. Proc. Acad. 1853, p. 279.

S. noveboracensis Forst., Cent. Ins. i, p. 17.

marginalis Fab., Ent. Syst. Mant. p. 215; Spec. Ins. i, p. 86; Oliv. Ent. ii, 11, p. 10, pl. 1, fig. 5; Herbst. Käfer v, p. 180; Lec. Proc. Acad. 1853, p. 278.

marginata Kby., Faun. Bor. Am. iv, p. 100.

S. americana Linn., Syst. Nat. ii, p. 570; Oliv. Ent. ii, 11, p. 1, fig. 9; Fab. Ent. Syst. i, p. 249; Syst. El. 1, p. 337; Hbst. Käfer v, p. 176.

peltatus Catesby, (*Scarabæus*) Nat. Hist. Carol. iii, pl. 10, fig. 7; Lec. Proc. Acad. 1853, p. 279.

affinis Kby., *terminata* Kby., Faun. Bor. Am. iv, p. 103.

canadensis Kby., loc. cit. p. 104.

S. ramosa Say, Journ. Acad. iii, p. 193; Lec. Proc. Acad. 1853, p. 279.

cervaria Mann., Bull. Mosc. 1843, ii, p. 252.

S. opaca Linn., Syst. Nat. ii, p. 571; Lec. Proc. Acad. 1866, p. 367.

S. bituberosa Lec., Col. Kans. 1859, p. 6.

NECROPHILUS Latr.

N. Pettitii n. sp.

subterraneus ‡ Horn, Trans. Am. Ent. Soc. 1868, p. 125.

N. hydrophiloides Mann., Bull. Mosc. 1843, ii, p. 253; Lac. Gen. Col. Atlas, pl. 16, fig. 5; Chevr. Guérin Icon. R. An. 61, pl. 17, fig. 12; Lec. Proc. Acad. 1853, p. 280.

ater Motsch., Bull. Mosc. 1845, iv, p. 363.

PELATES n. g.

P. latus Mann., (*Necrophilus*) 1852, ii, p. 331.

PTEROLOMA Gyll.

P. Forsstrœmi Gyll., Ins. Suecc. ii, p. 111; Duval, Gen. Col. Eur. pl. 34, fig. 169.

P. tenuicornis Lec., (*Necrophilus*) Proc. Acad. 1859, p. 84.

AGYRTES Fröhl.

A. longulus Lec., (*Necrophilus*) Proc. Acad. 1859, p. 282.

SPHÆRITES Dufts.

S. glabratus Fab., (*Hister*) Ent. Syst. i, p. 73; Sturm Ins. i, p. 264, pl. 20; Duval, Gen. Col. Eur. pl. 34, fig. 167.

politus Mann., Bull. Mosc. 1846, ii, p. 514.

LYROSOMA Mann.

L. opaca Mann., Bull. Mosc. 1853, iii, p. 175.

PINODYTES n. g.

P. cryptophagoides Mann., (*Catops*) Bull. Mosc. 1852, ii, p. 333.

PLATYCHOLEUS n. g.

P. leptinoides (*Ptomaph.*) Trans. Am. Ent. Soc. 1874, p. 77.

CATOPTRICHUS Murr.

C. Frankenhauseri Mann., (*Catops*) Bull. Mosc. 1852, ii, p. 332; Murray, Ann. Nat. Hist. 1856, p. 462.

CHOLEVA Latr.

C. egena n. sp.

C. luridipennis Mann., (*Catops*) Bull. Mosc. 1853, iii, p. 176; Murr. loc. cit. p. 305.

C. simplex Say, (*Catops*) Journ. Acad. v, p. 184; Lec. Proc. Acad. 1853, p. 281.

C. basillaris Say, (*Catops*) Journ. Acad. iii, p. 194; Murr. loc. cit. p. 394.

Spenciana Kby., Fauna Bor. Am. iv, p. 108; Murr. loc. cit. p. 304.

cadaverinus Mann., (*Catops*) Bull. Mosc. 1843, ii, p. 254.

brunnipennis Mann., (*Catops*) Bull. Mosc. 1853, iii, p. 176; Murr. loc. cit. p. 305.

C. clavicornis Lec., (*Catops*) Proc. Acad. 1853, p. 281.

C. decipiens n. sp.

C. terminans Lec., (*Catops*) Agass. Lake Super. p. 218; Proc. Acad. 1853, p. 282; Murr. loc. cit. p. 395.

PRIONOCHÆTA n. g.

P. opaca Say, (*Catops*) Journ. Acad. v, p. 184; Lec. Proc. Acad. 1853, p. 280; Murr. loc. cit. p. 395.

PTOMAPHAGUS Illig.

Pt. consobrinus Lec., Proc. Acad. 1853, p. 281; strigosus || Lec. loc. cit. Lecontei Murr., Mon. p. 459.

Pt. californicus Lec., loc. cit.; Murr. Mon. p. 458.

Pt. nevadicus n. sp.

Pt. oblitus Lec., loc. cit. p. 282.

Pt. pusio Lec., Proc. Acad. 1859, p. 282.

Catopomorphus Aubé.

Pt. parasitus Lec., Proc. Acad. 1853, p. 282.

Pt. brachyderus Lec., New Species, 1863, p. 25.

ADELOPS Tellkampf.

A. hirtus Tellk., Wiegm. Archiv. 1844, i, p. 318, pl. 8, figs. 1—6.

COLON Herbst.

C. bidentatum Sahlb., Ins. Fen. p. 95; Tournier, Ann. Ent. Soc. France, 1863, p. 137, pl. 4, fig. 2.

C. paradoxum Horn, n. sp.

C. Hubbardi Horn, n. sp.

C. dentatum Lec., Proc. Acad. 1853, p. 282.

C. celatum Horn, n. sp.

C. putum Horn, n. sp.

C. magnicolle Mann., Bull. Mosc. 1853, iii, p. 177.

C. pusillum Horn, n. sp.

C. clavatum Mann., Bull. Mosc. 1853, iii, p. 178.
C. inerme Mann., Bull. Mosc. 1852, ii, p. 333.
C. thoracicum Horn, n. sp.
C. asperatum Horn, n. sp.
C. nevadense Horn, n. sp.

TRIARTHRON Mærk.

T. Lecontei Horn, Trans. Amer. Ent. Soc. 1868, p. 131.

HYDNOBIUS Schmidt.

H. Matthewsii Crotch, Trans. Amer. Ent. Soc. 1874, p. 74.
? pallidum Say, (*Agathidium*) Journ. Acad. iv, p. 91.
H. strigilatus Horn, n. sp.
H. longulus Lec., Bull. U. S. Geol. Surv. 1879, vol. v, p. 511.
 longidens Lec., loc. cit. p. 511.
H. substriatus Lec., ♀ New Species, 1863, p. 25.
 curvidens Lec., ♂ Bull. Surv. loc. cit. p. 511.
H. latidens Lec., loc. cit. p. 512.
 pumilus Lec., loc. cit. p. 511.
H. obtusus Lec., loc. cit. p. 511.

ANOGDUS Lec.

A. capitatus Lec., Proc. Acad. 1866, p. 369.

ANISOTOMA Illiger.

A. alternata Mels., (*Leiodes*) Proc. Acad. ii, p. 103; Lec. Proc. Acad. 1853. p. 283.
A. humeralis Horn, n. sp.
A. valida Horn, n. sp.
A. assimilis Lec., Agass. Lake Super. p. 221; Proc. Acad. 1853, p. 283.
A. punctatostriata Kby., (*Leiodes*) Faun. Bor. Am. p. 110.
 indistincta Lec., Agass. Lake Super. p. 221; Proc. Acad. 1853, p. 283.
 læta Mann., Bull. Mosc. 1853, iii, p. 201.
A. difficilis Horn, n. sp.
A. collaris Lec., Agass. Lake Super. p. 221; Proc. Acad. 1853, p. 283.
A. curvata Mann., Bull. Mosc. 1853, iii, p. 202.
 morula Lec., Proc. Acad. 1859, p. 282.
A. conferta Lec., Proc. Acad. 1866, p. 367.
A. paludicola Crotch, Trans. Am. Ent. Soc. 1874, p. 74.
A. strigata Lec., Agass. Lake Super. p. 221; Proc. Acad. 1853. p. 284.
A. obsoleta Mels., (*Pallodes*) Proc. Acad. ii, p. 107; Lec. Proc. Acad. 1853, p. 284.
A. ecarinata Horn, n. sp.
A. lateritia Mann., Bull. Mosc. 1852, ii, p. 245, (not identified).

COLENIS Erichs.

C. impunctata Lec., Proc. Acad. 1853, p. 284.

CYRTUSA Erichs.

C. picipennis Lec., (*Amphicyllis*) New Spec. 1863, p. 25; Proc. Acad. 1866, p. 369.
C. blandissima Zimm., Trans. Am. Ent. Soc. 1869, p. 250.
C. egena Lec., Proc. Acad. 1853, p. 284.
 impubis Zimm., loc. cit. p. 251.

ISOPLASTUS n. g.

I. fossor Horn, n. sp.

LIODES Latr.

L. globosa Lec., (*Cyrtusa*) Agass. Lake Super. p. 222; Proc. Acad. 1853, p. 285.

L. polita Lec., Proc. Acad. 1853, p. 285.

L. discolor Mels., Proc. Acad. ii, p. 103.

L. Blanchardi Horn, n. sp.

L. obsoleta Horn, n. sp.

L. basalis Lec., loc. cit. p. 285.

   var. *dichroa* Lec., loc. cit.

L. geminata Horn, n. sp.

L. confusa Horn, n. sp.

AGATHIDIUM Illig.

A. oniscoides Beauv., Ins. Afr. et Am. p. 160, pl. 6, fig. 2; Lec. Proc. Acad. 1853, p. 285.

   piceum Mels., Proc. Acad. 1844, p. 103.

   globatile Lec., Proc. Amer. Philos. Soc. 1878, p. 598.

A. exiguum Mels. loc. cit. p. 103.

   ruficorne Lec., Agass. Lake Super. p. 222.

A. dentigerum Horn, n. sp.

A. californicum Horn, n. sp.

A. revolvens Lec., Agass. Lake Super. p. 222; Proc. Acad. 1853, p. 286.

A. sexstriatum Horn, n. sp.

A. bistriatum Horn, n. sp.

A. estriatum Horn, n. sp.

A. repentinum Horn, n. sp.

A. concinnum Mann., Bull. Mosc. 1852, ii, p. 370.

   effluens Mann., Bull. Mosc. 1853, iii, p. 202.

A. rotundulum Mann., Bull. Mosc. 1852, ii, p. 370.

A. angulare Mann., loc. cit. p. 369.

A. politum Lec., Proc. Acad. 1866, p. 370.

   parvulum Lec., Proc. Amer. Philos. Soc. 1878, p. 598.

A. pulchrum Lec., Proc. Acad. 1853, p. 286.

   mandibulatum Mann., Bull. Mosc. 1853, iii, p. 203.

A. difforme Lec., (*Phalacrus*) Agass. Lake Super. p. 222; Proc. Acad. 1853, p. 286.

AGLYPTUS Lec.

A. lævis Lec., (? *Colenis*) Proc. Acad. 1853, p. 284; Proc. Acad. 1866, p. 369.

EMPELUS Lec.

E. brunnipennis Mann., (*Litochrus*) Bull. Mosc. 1852, ii, p. 369; Lec. Class. Coleop. N. A. 1861, p. 52.

CALYPTOMERUS Redt.

C. oblongulus Mann., (*Clambus*) Bull. Mosc. 1853, iii, p. 203; Lec. loc. cit.

CLAMBUS Fischer.

C. gibbulus Lec., (*Sternuchus*) Agass. Lake Super. p. 222; Proc. Acad. 1853, p. 286.

C. puberulus Lec., New Species, 1863, p. 26.

C. vulneratus Lec., Bull. U. S. Geol. Surv. 1879, vol. v, p. 512.

C. seminulum Horn, n. sp.

Synonymical list of the genera of Silphidæ based on the notes in the preceding pages.

Tribe SILPHINI.

Necrophorus Fab.

Silpha Linn.

Necrodes Leach.

Ptomaphila Hope. (a)

Necrophilus Latr.

Pelates Horn.

Pteroloma Gyll. (b)

Apatetica Hope.

Agyrtes Fröhl.

Sphærites Duftsch.

Tribe LYROSOMINI.

Lyrosoma Mann.

Tribe PINODYTINI.

Pinodytes Horn.

Tribe CHOLEVINI.

Group BATHYSCIÆ.

Leptodirus Sturm. (a)

S. G. *Propus* Abeille.

Antrocharis Abeille.

S. G. *Diaprysius* Abeille.

Oryotus Miller.

Aphaobius Abeille.

Adelops ‡ Schauf.

Pholeuon Hampe.

S. G. *Drimeotus* Miller.

Bathyscia Schiœdte.

Adelops ‡ Auct. Europ.

Quæstus Schauf.

Quæsticulus Schauf.

Cytodromus Abeille. (c)

Spelæochlamys Dieck. (c)

Group PLATYCHOLEI.

Platycholeus Horn.

Group CHOLEVÆ.

Catoptrichus Murray.

Choleva Latr. (a)

Prionochæta Horn.

Ptomaphagus Illig.

S. G. *Catopomorphus* Aubé.

Adelops Tellk.

Group COLONES.

Colon Herbst.

Camiarus Sharp.

Tribe ANISOTOMINI.

Triarthron Mærkel.

Stereus Woll.

Hydnobius Schmidt.

Dietta Sharp.

Anogdus Lec.

Anisotoma Illig.

Colenis Erichs.

Agaricophagus Schmidt.

Liodes Latr.

Scotocryptus Girard. (d)

Cyrtusa Erichs.

Amphicyllis Erichs.

Isoplastus Horn.

Agathidium Illig.

Aglyptus Lec.

Tribe CLAMBINI.

Empelus Lec.

Calyptomerus Redt.

Clambus Fisch.

Loricaster Muls.

(a) For synonymy already published see "Catalogus."
(b) See "Catalogus," excluding *Lyrosoma*.
(c) Of uncertain position and value.
(d) Possibly allied to *Aglyptus* but undoubtedly an Anisotomide.

EXPLANATION OF PLATE V.

Fig. 1.—*Necrophorus carolinus* Linn.
Fig. 2.—Thorax beneath of *N. marginatus* Fab. ·
Fig. 3.—*Silpha surinamensis* Fab.
Fig. 4.—*S. bituberosa* Lec.; *a*, thorax beneath of same.
Fig. 5.—*Necrophilus hydrophiloides* Mann.
Fig. 6.—*Pelates latus* Mann.; *a*, thorax beneath of same.
Fig. 7.—*Pteroloma tenuicornis* Lec.
Fig. 8.—*Apatetica lebioides* Westw., (after Lacordaire.*)
Fig. 9.—*Agyrtes longulus* Lec.
Fig. 10.—*Sphærites glabratus* Fab.
Fig. 11.—*Lyrosoma opacum* Mann.
Fig. 12.--*Pinodytes cryptophagoides* Mann.; *b*, antenna of same.
Fig. 13.—*Catoptrichus Frankenhæuseri* Mann.; *a*, anterior tibia ♂; *b*, antenna.
Fig. 14.—*Prionochæta opaca* Say; *a*, tibial spur.
Fig. 15.—*Ptomaphagus consobrinus* Lec.; *a*, antenna.
Fig. 16.—*Ptomaphagus* (Catopomorphus) *brachyderus* Lec.; *a*, antenna.
Fig. 17.—*Choleva luridipennis* Mann.; *a*, thorax beneath of same.

CORRECTIONS.

Page 235, line 4 from bottom, for terse read tense.

Page 307, line 21, for simple read single.

The genus *Camiarus* Sharp, is written as in the original description *Camirus* in the earlier pages. Dr. Sharp subsequently changed the latter name from its resemblance to *Camira*.

---

* Occurs in the Himalaya region of India.

EXPLANATION OF PLATE VI.

Fig. 1.—*Adelops hirtus* Tellk.; *a*, head seen from the front showing the eyes.

Fig. 2.—*Platycholeus leptinoides* Crotch.

Fig. 3.—*Bathyscia Freyeri** Miller.

Fig. 4.—*Pholeuon leptoderum** Friw.; *a*, thorax beneath of same.

Fig. 5.—*Oryotus Schmidtii** Miller.

Fig. 6.—*Leptoderus Hohenwarti** Schmidt; *a, b*, thorax and body beneath of same.

Fig. 7.—*Colon thoracicum* Horn; *a*, antenna of same.

Fig. 8.—*C. magnicolle* Mann.

Fig. 9.—Antenna of *C. bidentatum* Sahlb.

Fig. 10.—Anterior and posterior legs of *C. bidentatum* ♂; *a*, anterior tibial spur enlarged; *b*, posterior tibial spur; *c*, anterior tibial spur of a male of *C. inerme*.

Fig. 11.—Anterior and posterior legs of *C. dentatum* ♂.

Fig. 12.—Same of *C. celatum* ♂.

Fig. 13.—Same of *C. Hubbardi* ♂.

Fig. 14.—Anterior tibia and posterior leg of *C. paradoxum* ♂.

Fig. 15.—*Triarthron Lecontei* Horn; *a*, antenna; *b*, posterior leg of ♂.

Fig. 16.—*Hydnobius Matthewsii* Crotch.

Fig. 17.—Posterior leg of *H. obtusus* Lec. ♂.

Fig. 18.—Anterior leg of *H. strigilatus* Horn, ♂.

Fig. 19.—Posterior leg of *H. substriatus* Lec. ♂, with variation.

Fig. 20.—Same of *H. longulus* Lec. ♂, with variation.

Fig. 21.—Same of *H. latidens* Lec. ♂.

Fig. 22.—*Anogdus capitatus* Lec.; *a*, antenna; *b*, posterior leg.

Fig. 23.—*Colenis impunctata* Lec.

Fig. 24.—*Camiarus thoracicus* † Sharp.

Fig. 25.—*C. convexus* † Sharp.

---

* These occur in various caves of Europe.

† These occur in New Zealand.

www.ingramcontent.com/pod-product-compliance
Lightning Source LLC
Chambersburg PA
CBHW030551270326
41927CB00008B/1600